Identifying Training Needs

Tom Boydell and Malcolm Leary

Tom Boydell, a graduate in engineering, worked with VSO in Guyana, where he became interested in learning and development within organisations. After obtaining postgraduate qualifications, including a Ph.D. in management learning, he spent 20 years as principal lecturer at Sheffield Hallam University, responsible for postgraduate programmes in HRM and organisation development and learning. He then established his own companies, The Learning Company Project and Transform, for which he researches, writes, and consults, working with clients throughout Europe, North and South America, and Africa. The author of over 30 books on management and organisational learning, he also holds external teaching and research appointments at a number of universities, and is a member of the Society for Research into Adult Development and a founder member of the Association for Social Development.

Malcolm Leary's career as a consultant, researcher, and writer began in the steel industry in the 1960s. Later he worked for a number of training boards before co-founding Transform – an international consultancy specialising in individual and organisation development. He currently has clients in both the private and public sectors in the UK, Spain, and South Africa. His research interests include conflict-handling, teamworking, and organisational learning, leading to the design of a number of major integrated development programmes, including first line management, developing developers and personal effectiveness. He claims his own main source of learning comes from singing with a championship male voice choir.

Other learning and development titles published by the CIPD include:

Creating a Training and Development Strategy (2nd ed) Andrew Mayo

Cultivating Self-Development David Megginson and Vivien Whitaker

Delivering Training Suzy Siddons

Designing Training Alison Hardingham

Developing Effective Training Skills Tony Pont

Evaluating Training (2nd ed) Peter Bramley

Facilitation Skills Frances and Roland Bee

Introduction to Training Penny Hackett

Psychology for Trainers Alison Hardingham

The Chartered Institute of Personnel and Development is the leading publisher of books and reports for personnel and training professionals, students, and all those concerned with the effective management and development of people at work. For full details of all our titles, please contact the Publishing Department:
tel. 020-8612 6204
e-mail publish@cipd.co.uk
The catalogue of all CIPD titles can be viewed on the CIPD website:
www.cipd.co.uk/bookstore

IDENTIFYING
TRAINING
NEEDS

Tom Boydell and Malcolm Leary

Chartered Institute of Personnel and Development

First published in 1996
Reprinted in 1996, 1998, 1999, 2000, 2003 (twice), 2005

Design and typesetting by Paperweight
Printed in Great Britain by
The Cromwell Press, Trowbridge, Wiltshire

British Library Cataloguing in Publication Data
A catalogue record for this book is available from the
British Library

ISBN
0-85292-630-8

Chartered Institute of Personnel and Development, 151 The Broadway,
London SW19 1JQ
Tel.: 020 8612 6200
E-mail: cipd@cipd.co.uk   Website: www.cipd.co.uk
Incorporated by Royal Charter. Registered charity no. 1079797

Contents

Introduction to the Identification of Training Needs

Why bother to identify training needs?

This book is not based on the assumption that all training is necessarily and inevitably a good thing. In most organisations today resources are scarce and have to be used carefully time is of the essence, and trainers of all kinds are required to justify their position and account for their activities. Whether you are involved in training as a full-time professional or as a practising manager with responsibility for training and developing your staff, the same disciplines apply.

Training that is ill-directed and inadequately focused does not serve the purposes of the trainers, the learner, or the organisation. This book aims to provide trainers with the framework, tools, techniques, processes, and skills to take appropriate first steps in designing and implementing efficient, effective, timely, and productive training for those who need it most. It emphasises the importance of building a good foundation by clearly and precisely identifying and analysing the needs that the training will address.

Identification of training needs (ITN), if done properly, provides the basis on which all other training activities can be considered. Although requiring careful thought and analysis, it is a process that needs to be carried out with sensitivity: people's learning is important to them, and the success of the organisation may be at stake.

It is important to know exactly what you are doing, and

why, when undertaking ITN. This is the reason we have included material to help you make considered decisions and take thoughtful actions. You will find, however, that the return on the investment you make in fully understanding what ITN is all about will make it well worth while.

Some basic assumptions

Because the rest of this book is built around certain beliefs and assumptions about organisations, the people who work in them, and what good training practices are about, it is important to be clear about these from the start. They look something like this:

Assumptions about the organisation	Assumptions about people
1 The organisation has objectives that it wants to achieve for the benefit of all stakeholders or members, including owners, employees, customers, suppliers, and neighbours.	1 People have aspirations; they want to develop and to learn new abilities and use them.
2 These objectives can be achieved only through harnessing the abilities of its people, releasing potential and maximising opportunities for development.	2 In order to learn and use new abilities, people need appropriate opportunities, resources, and conditions.
3 Therefore people must know what they need to learn in order to achieve organisational goals.	3 Therefore, to meet people's aspirations, the organisation must provide effective and attractive learning resources and conditions.

4 There needs therefore to be a match between achieving organisational goals and providing attractive learning opportunities.

A number of important consequences follow from point 4. If our aim is to ensure that learning opportunities match closely the aims and goals of the organisation, then an effective ITN process enables us to do this. It will then be possible to achieve our other training objectives, viz:

■   to make learning opportunities 'effective and attractive'. This is what training design and delivery and implementation are about

∎ to keep a constant check on how far this match is being effectively continued. This is what training evaluation is about.

So, in a nutshell, we need good ITN processes in order to provide the learning opportunities required to achieve the goals of the organisation.

Is the converse true? Should we ensure that we provide only those learning opportunities that directly help to achieve the goals of the organisation? On the face of it the answer might appear to be 'yes'. However, some well-known companies are putting considerable resources into employee development programmes, where employees are encouraged to learn skills that, at first sight, appear to have nothing to do with their job performance as such. A famous example is Rover, where, through the Rover Learning Business, all members of the group are given personal learning budgets that can be used for learning virtually anything, job-related or not. Indeed, the more directly job-related the learning, the less likely it is that authority will be given to spend one's personal budget on it, because job-related learning is seen as something that should be part of the direct job-related training provision. So how does this match up to 'meeting the organisation's objectives'?

When launching the Rover Learning Business, Chairman Graham Day said that 'By encouraging continuous learning and development among all our employees, they will start to question more and more the way we manage things.' So the link is there, but over a long time-scale. In effect, the sequence of thinking was:

∎ In order to achieve our objectives we need our people to question the way we do things.

∎ Therefore our people need to learn to question the way we do things.

The 'training need' was about learning to question 'the

way we do things'. The solution was not direct training in questioning, but a subtler, longer-term process of encouraging employees to take an active involvement in their own development, thus increasing their commitment to learning, to their work, and to the organisation as a whole.

Before looking in some detail at what we mean by 'learning', it will first be useful to consider how the concepts of 'training need' and ITN have evolved over recent decades.

The history of ITN

Approaches to ITN have gradually changed over the past 35 years, following a pattern of long-term problem-solving first identified by Pedler, Burgoyne and Boydell (1996).

This pattern starts with a problem, P_1, to which a solution, S_1, is found. In the course of training and ITN, the progression over 35 years has been as follows:

Problem

P₁ (1950–60):
Shortage of skilled employees
(operators and craftworkers).

Solution

↘

S₁ (1960–70): *Systematic training*
Emphasis on job analysis, precise identification of job or task needs, behavioural objectives, programme planning, systematic evaluation.

P₂ (1970–75):   ↙
Emphasis on S₁ led to a number of problems, including these factors:

▪ The focus was too narrow – on jobs, not people.

▪ Jobs could not be split between microskills and then got together again. Hence a problem of 'transfer training'.

▪ Preparation of job descriptions and training-needs analyses often became an end in itself, encouraged by grant schemes from industrial training boards. Led to training bureaucracies.

▪ Job analysis approaches were not appropriate for jobs that required discretion and judgement – such as management jobs.

▪ The standardisation inherent in analytical approaches did not take into account essential differences between people and the diversity of gender, race, and age which affect the way the work was viewed and the job done.

▪ The emphasis was on how the job was being done at that time. Any scope for making improvements or being more creative and innovative was not really considered. Thus there was a danger of becoming very skilled and competent, but at yesterday's skills – especially in situations of rapid change (which applied in many situations, the days of stability being over).

S_2 (1975–85):
Two main streams appeared in response to these difficulties and limitations; one brought the individual and the personal much more into the calculations, and the other focused attention on learning from doing things. So we had:

▪ *self-development*, where people were encouraged to look at the influence of their personality, inclinations, and preferences in relation to the job. This was then taken into consideration when designing training. Programmes for self-development were often run in groups.

▪ *action learning*, again in the form of groups coming together to carry out projects at work (ie the 'action'), discuss their activities with others, take further action, and identify what they have learned from this (ie the learning).

P_3 (1985–90):
At least two significant problems arose:

- Action learning and self-development were reserved almost entirely for managers. Operator-level workers still received only systematic training.

- Both these approaches were primarily individual-orientated, with little consideration for the development of the organisation as a whole.

S_3 (1990–95):
A number of approaches evolved, including:

- *continuous improvement*, action learning for operations workers

- *employee development*, or self-development for everybody (as in the Rover Learning Business)

- *competencies, NVQs and portfolio assessment*, keeping elements of systematic training but closing the gap between learning–doing–assessing.

- *the learning company*, an overarching concept to integrate all the above.

P_4 (date?):
We do not yet know what this will be. Perhaps it will emerge as something to do with responsibility to the environment and to the community. Perhaps it will be about ethics, or cross-cultural working.

S_4 ???:
Working across boundaries? Generally working and learning together outside the organisation, just as much as inside? With a much wider range of stakeholders?

Of course, all the solutions (S_1 to S_3) possess, and retain, their strengths. In this book we shall seek to combine the best elements of each, linking (wherever possible) individual and organisational needs, emphasising the importance of connecting working and learning, and considering the contrasting needs of people as individuals and the requirements of the work they do.

Above all, organisations need people who perform at required levels and to necessary standards. If we focus on what performance is required and how this translates itself into training needs we shall be taking an important first step in effective ITN. We shall examine the background to these issues in the next section, using recent research findings as our guide.

Levels of performance and need

We find it helpful to consider performance (whether of people, systems, processes, teams, or the organisation as a whole) at three different levels. This means that the needs arising from these levels of performance will also be different. The three levels of performance, and hence levels of need, are:

Level 1   Implementing (I_1) – doing things well

Level 2   Improving (I_2) – doing things better

Level 3   Innovating (I_3) – doing new and better things

We shall now explain what we mean by these terms.

Performance and needs at level 1

Implementing-level needs arise where the main problem is the gap between desired and actual performance. In other words, this is where people need to learn how to do the job well – as defined by current standards. It is about learning to satisfy basic requirements and needs, in order to bring performance up to standard and maintain it there.

Performance and needs at level 2

Obviously, level 1 needs are, in a way, about improving individual or group performance that is currently lagging behind. However, when we refer to needs at level 2, we are talking about improving the performance of everybody – of the organisation as a whole – by raising current standards. This is where *continuous improvement* comes in – where we look at what we as an organisation are doing and make systematic, organisation-wide improvements so as to do it better, ie more efficiently and economically.

Performance and needs at level 3

This represents a still further level of improvement – making a step-change rather than one that is continuous or incremental. This can be done only by a thorough review of all our processes and of how they are interrelated, based on a review of our purpose – why we do what we do. What are we trying to achieve?

It must be stressed that these levels are additive, ie

■   to make successful improvements we need to learn at level 2 and then implement (level 1) the improvements

■   to be successful in innovation we need to learn at level 3 and then implement (level 1) the new methods and continuously improve (level 2) them.

This is shown diagrammatically in Figure 1.

Figure 1
THE ADDITIVE NATURE OF THE THREE LEVELS OF PERFORMANCE

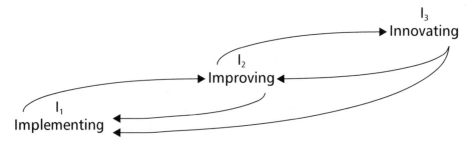

Modes of learning at each level of performance

Our recent research has shown that at each of the three levels of performance different learning modes are involved. Careful consideration needs therefore to be given to how training is designed and implemented, in order to deliver the business benefits required from each performance level. In the following section we consider these different modes of learning.

I_1: *implementing*

Remembering that we are here concerned with 'doing things well', this calls for basic learning in terms of the following modes.

> *Mode 1 – adhering*, ie learning to carry out basic tasks correctly. This is done by sticking closely to the rules laid down for doing the job and following precisely the set procedures. For example, this way of working or performing is essential whenever safety or health factors are involved. Driving a car, or flying a passenger aeroplane, come to mind. Airline pilots do everything 'by the book', using extensive check-lists of procedures that have been prepared for every contingency.

> *Mode 2 – adapting*, when we may need to bend the rules slightly and make adjustments to procedures in order to make things work better. There may be minor changes in work circumstances as the job is being carried out, many of them relatively unpredictable – situations rarely remain exactly the same and we can plan ahead to a certain degree only. When unpredictable things do happen we may need to discover short cuts and make minor alterations to make things work more effectively. Trial-and-error methods are used to find these short cuts, and they may need to be made on the spot.

> *Mode 3 – relating*, involves learning to understand why things have been set up the way they have and why procedures work as they do – as well as appreciating what needs to be done. In performing the task in the prescribed way there will be certain reasons, customs,

norms, and conventions covering the way we are required to behave, whom we should talk to (and about what and when), and how we are to deal with other people involved. We call this *relating* because it involves fitting in with established ways.

We note that modes 1, 2, and 3 (*adhering*, *adapting* and *relating*) are the focus of most basic instruction and training, whether designed for newcomers to the work or to 'get people up to scratch' if their individual performance has failed to match the standard required, or if for some other reason they are lagging behind.

I_2: *improving*

For I_2 performance, where our aim is 'to do things better', different types of learning are needed. This level requires (in addition to modes 1, 2, and 3) an ability to act more independently, to take initiatives, and to make your own meaning and sense out of what is going on. So we are concerned with the following modes.

> *Mode 4 – experiencing*, ie being able to reflect on experiences and make our own meaning from them. This results in an enhanced ability to translate personal understanding and meaning into actions consistent with whatever lessons we have learned. We become much more aware of our preferred ways of doing things and of what works best for us in a variety of different situations, and are more confident in taking initiatives – 'doing things our way'.

Initiatives and new actions have to be carried through in a proper manner – and normally involve other people whom we have to take along with us. I_2 performance therefore requires, in addition to mode 4, a further set of learning:

> *Mode 5 – experimenting*, ie learning to design and carry out systematic processes, in the form of experiments, in order consciously to discover more about the job and the work, normally in terms of particular target areas deemed in need of improving. From the resulting

insights and greater understanding about what works (and what does not) we can design, test, and evaluate new methods, procedures, and better ways of working. So, for example, the procedures that airline pilots use in mode 1 are devised by thorough testing and experimentation in mode 5.

If people are encouraged to learn in these ways (ie modes 4 and 5) considerable improvements can be made and performance enhanced.

For example, a group of first line managers were involved in a work-based learning programme in a sawmill, working as a learning group. They instituted job improvements that eventually resulted in positive changes being made. The return on this learning investment made the effort well worth while:

■ Forty-seven per cent fewer lighting units were used, together with less electricity, which saving considerably increased the efficiency of the lighting system.

■ By improving staffing arrangements on the telephone switchboard, £9,000 a year was saved

■ £48,000 was saved each year by changing the design and operation of the stock control system.

So there was a direct, immediate, and measurable link between training and business performance.

These kinds of improvements can be achieved in any sector. In one NHS region, learning in modes 4 and 5 led first to increased initiative-taking; staff looked around for improvements to be made, communication was improved, people worked together better, commitment was higher and staff morale increased. This led in turn to measurable savings in terms of take-up of post-natal examinations (17 per cent increase); fewer errors in referral entries (70 per cent reduction); shorter hip-replacement hospital stay (reduced to three days); shorter patient waiting times (reduced by 31 per cent); and greater surgical services activity (increased by 20 per cent).

I_3: *innovating*

Performance at this level requires two sets of learning in addition to modes 1 to 5. Here we are concerned with doing 'new and better things', and therefore learning has to concentrate on a more sophisticated and complex set of factors.

Mode 6 – connecting, ie making connections between things, events, and people, and allowing integration and synergy to be achieved. Because the things that various groups of people do are brought together, the whole becomes greater than the sum of the parts (rather than, as so often, less!). In this way we work across boundaries (between jobs, departments, and teams); we become more aware of our own position and that of others; and we examine our assumptions and the self-imposed limits these may be causing. We thus learn to work better with others, and particularly with people from different disciplines, who may have different perspectives and assumptions, all of which need accommodating.

Mode 6 requires us to learn to see the whole situation, to think holistically and systemically, and to recognise important patterns, sequences, and connections – to see where things depend on one another. We can thus look more closely at the implications and consequences of actions, and be more careful and sensitive – recognising, and working within, the broader context of what we are doing. All in all this is quite a different kind of learning from that in modes 1 to 5.

Mode 7 – dedicating, where we learn to work out of a sense of purpose – why we are doing something, and why we are doing it at a certain time and in a particular way. This should mean that we develop a clear sense of 'what is in it' not just for ourselves but for our colleagues, the organisation as a whole, and, possibly, the wider community.

Major business benefits can arise from learning at this level – learning to do new and better things by adding modes 6 and 7 to our repertoire.

The BICC telephone cable factory in Manchester was faced with a major crisis: falling sales, lower prices, and heavy losses, all in the context of a shrinking UK market. One quite sensible course of action would have been to close down the plant, but it was decided to keep it open and to switch to a team-working structure. This involved numerous 'training' changes, including:

- careful selection of teamleaders (there were 23 in all, seven on each of three shifts, plus two on day-times only)
- training teamleaders in a wide range of management skills, emphasising the need to think for oneself (mode 4), carry out systematic improvements (mode 5), and work with team-leaders on other shifts and in other manufacturing process areas (mode 6)
- helping teamleaders to identify for themselves the skills they felt they needed (modes 4 and 7)
- using all the above training to acquire National Vocational Qualifications (NVQs) in management
- training entire teams to think for themselves, make systematic improvements, and work well together and with other teams (modes 4 to 6)
- multiskilling training of team members in cable-making methods (modes 1 to 4)
- providing teamleaders and members with resources for non-job-related personal development (modes 1 to 7)
- encouraging and allowing teamleaders and team members to meet with middle and senior managers to put forward suggestions and ideas and receive feedback (modes 4 to 7)

∎ taking teamleaders on visits to companies in other industries (modes 4 to 6).

At the same time, lots of other changes were made to support the initiative. The wages system was revised, consolidating 32 different rates into a unified single-status package. At the same time the middle management structure was made much flatter by taking out one layer and appointing three shift managers. A senior management team was formed from all departmental heads and was led by a new general manager (appointed from outside) with a reputation of being able to manage major change programmes successfully.

The factory site had become run down and therefore a number of major building works, refurbishments, layout alterations, and general upgradings of facilities were carried out. (The main machinery and plant items and ancillary services had been upgraded some time before and therefore did not need further investment.) Of particular importance was the introduction of on-site team rooms, which quickly became used for communal refreshment and meal breaks, team meetings, information display, and IT centres, providing teams with production data and hitherto 'secret' commercial information.

The overall effects on business results – ie the benefit of the training and other changes to the business – were dramatic. Only nine months after the teamworking initiative was started the effects were measurable, and included productivity rises by 113 per cent; scrap costs falling by 50 per cent; lead times drastically reduced; absenteeism falling by 58 per cent; on-time deliveries the best ever, at 98 per cent; UK market share risen from 17 per cent to 40 per cent; new export markets opened up; and contracts won. Overall the plant moved from making severe losses to significant profits and, by not closing down, 300 jobs were saved.

When is a training need not a training need?

Clearly the BICC case involved some changes that had nothing to do with training (eg improving the working environment); others, such as multiskilling, *were* 'training', in the sense of systematically instructing people in skills and knowledge; and yet others lay somewhere in between, such as helping teams to learn to work with others, which involved a form of group-counselling rather than instruction as such. This is in fact typical of development at the creative level. For this to work well there will inevitably need to be a whole range of interventions, including basic instruction and learning, improvements in systems, and introducing better ways of doing things – all linked together.

The more that business benefits and performance enhancements are required, the greater the range of learning methods and approaches that we shall need to employ. Figure 2 shows that the *scope* of changes needs to be widened if performance at I_2 and I_3 is to be enhanced.

Figure 2

THE RELATIONSHIP BETWEEN LEVELS OF PERFORMANCE AND THE VARIETY OF REQUIRED INTERVENTIONS

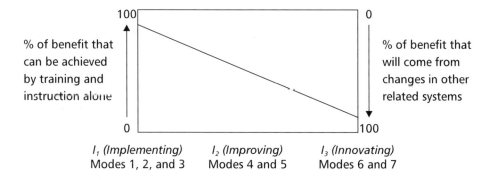

% of benefit that can be achieved by training and instruction alone

% of benefit that will come from changes in other related systems

I_1 *(Implementing)* Modes 1, 2, and 3 I_2 *(Improving)* Modes 4 and 5 I_3 *(Innovating)* Modes 6 and 7

Of course, the exact shape and positioning of the line in Figure 2 differs from organisation to organisation, but the principle is quite clear. Modes 1 to 3 can be learned mainly by instruction. Modes 6 and 7 require very significant changes in other systems and processes as well, whereas modes 4 and 5 lie somewhere in between.

Other versions of this simple graph can be drawn. One may be illustrated by a simple story from a major international travel company, where an internal consultant was describing the responses of two sections – training and quality improvement – to a manager's query: 'What can you offer my department?' The training section responded with a menu of syllabuses and courses. The quality people, on the other hand, said that they had a whole range of intervention processes, of which training was just one, that could be applied directly to the work setting. Could they come and talk further about what was required?

The point of the story is that at the *implementing* level, with its emphasis on *content*, syllabuses and courses are often quite appropriate. *Improving* calls for the ability to design and implement appropriate *processes* for learning and change. And *innovating* involves changing the *context* by creating a wide range of new interconnected systems and relationships. So we have here another version of the same diagram – Figure 3.

Figure 3

THE RELATIONSHIP BETWEEN LEVELS OF PERFORMANCE AND THE SEPARATION OF WORKING/LEARNING

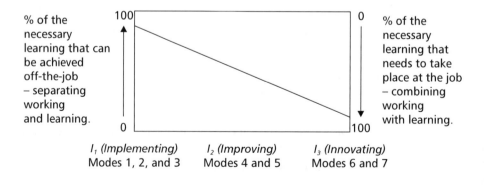

Mode	Description	Learning processes	Help by Others
I₁: IMPLEMENTING			
Mode 1 *Adhering*	Learning to do things 'correctly', sticking to rules, procedures, and laid-down ways of doing things	Instruction, drill, rote learning, memory games, practice with feedback results	Tell people what to do Give feedback of results Allow time for practice Act as role model yourself for adhering to rules and procedures
Mode 2 *Adapting*	Learning to modify rules, procedures, and methods, discovering short cuts and modifications to make them work better	Observation of effects of *ad hoc* trial-and-error adjustments	Support *ad hoc* changes Act as role model yourself for adaptation
Mode 3 *Relating*	Learning to understand established 'correct' explanations of why things are as they are, why they work as they do, and internalising the ways things 'ought' to be done	Expository teaching; going from known to unknown, concrete to abstract, particular to general, simple to complex; summarising, testing, understanding	Explain why and how things work and are done Encourage questions Ask questions to elicit level of understanding Act as role model yourself for relating to established ways and norms
I₂: IMPROVING			
Mode 4 *Experiencing*	Learning to make one's own meaning from experiences, from things that happen, creating or discovering one's own understanding	Having experiences, reflecting, forming new ideas, trying out	Provide variety of experiences Encourage reflection Ask questions to cause others to think through their own ideas Act as role model yourself for learning from own experiences
Mode 5 *Experimenting*	Learning to find out, in a systematic way, more about something by hypothesising, carrying out carefully planned experiments or pilot projects, and analysing and reviewing the results of these	Systematically structuring experiences – using continuous improvement tools such as surveys, flow charts, brainstorming, fishbones, Pareto, nominal group technique, correlation analysis, and control charts	Support initiatives Provide opportunities for systematic experimentation Support training in systematic improvement techniques Be receptive to new ideas Act as coach, mentor, facilitator Act as role model yourself for continuous improvement
I₃: INNOVATING			
Mode 6 *Connecting*	Learning to see systematically – wholes, connections, patterns, interdependencies – hence to empathise, identify with others, and acknowledge and value diversity	Reflecting, seeking patterns, themes, assumptions, dialogue, relationship-mapping, role negotiation, continuous improvement tools	Support training in dialogue, assumption-checking and other holistic techniques Encourage and support establishment of autonomous teams Support autonomous teams by making clear they are indeed autonomous Act as coach, mentor, facilitator Act as role model yourself for holistic approach
Mode 7 *Dedicating*	Learning to recognise and commit oneself to one's purpose in life in the sense of joining with others to do something in and for the external world	Biography work, U-procedure, whole-system interventions	Support individual, team and organisation biography work, U-procedures, whole-system interventions Act as role model yourself for sense of purpose

Table 1

LEVELS OF PERFORMANCE, MODES OF LEARNING AND LEARNING PROCESSES

In fact, the nature of appropriate learning intervention will be very different at each of the three levels. This is beyond the direct scope of this book, but Table 1 (on page 17) gives some indication of what might be involved. Table 2, meanwhile, summarises some areas of benefit at each of these three levels of performance and need.

Table 2

BUSINESS BENEFITS AT THE THREE LEVELS OF PERFORMANCE

	LEVEL OF NEED – PERFORMANCE		
	Level 1	Level 2	Level 3
Business areas and possible benefits	*Implementing:* Doing things well	*Improving:* Doing things better	*Innovating:* Doing new and better things
Organisational processes	Successful implemention of systems	Improvement of and efficiency of systems	Better strategy for choosing which systems to use
Marketing	Matching the competition Satisfying customers	Beating the competition Delighting customers	Growing the market Engaging customers
Legislation	Meeting the requirements	Improving on the requirements	Creating the requirements
Technology	Introducing technology effectively	Using technology more efficiently	Developing your own new technology
Government initiatives (eg Investors in People)	Meeting the standards (Getting the award)	Exceeding the standards	Setting new standards
Relationships	Businesslike relationships and behaviour	Collaborative relationships and behaviour	Creative new relationships and behaviour
Individual aspirations	Meeting minimum career qualifications and requirements	Moving along a career path	Carrying your own career forward

Organisational, group, and individual needs

As well as the three *levels* of need – implementing, improving, and innovating (I_1, I_2 and I_3) – there are also three *areas* of need: organisational, group, and individual. Because we shall be devoting specific chapters to each of these, at this point we shall give only a quick overview of them.

Organisational needs

These concern the performance of the organisation as a whole. Information about this overall performance may identify areas of need either for training or other interventions.

I_1: implementing level

Here ITN is about finding out whether the organisation is meeting its current performance standards and objectives, and , if not, exploring ways in which training or learning might help it to do so.

> A shoe manufacturing company in the Midlands recognised that it was not reaching its quarterly output targets.
>
> A car distribution network wanted to increase the percentage of customers retained.
>
> Through the use of a simple questionnaire a hotel found out that only 35 per cent of its guests rated the standard of service higher than 'fair'.

In these cases further investigation was then necessary to ascertain whether or not training might help; we shall look at how to do this in Chapters 4 and 5.

I_2: improving level

Organisational needs arise at this level when we want not just to meet current objectives but, for various reasons, to raise their level.

A hospital trust fund was proud of the effective way it carried out hip-replacement operations, with an outstanding success rate and a very short patient waiting-list. However, it discovered that the cost of carrying out these operations was the highest in the country, such that its annual budget was spent in only eight months. It had to find ways of carrying out the operations more efficiently, as well as effectively.

Spares-R-Us car exhaust and tyre suppliers and fitters prided itself on its value-for-money service. However, its market share began to drop. Investigation showed that the main competitor, although marginally more expensive, was able to supply and fit tyres in only three-quarters of the time that Spares-R-Us could achieve, and customers were willing to pay that little bit more if it meant less hanging around waiting. Spares-R-Us therefore had to shorten the overall fitting time while keeping costs down.

I_3: innovating
level

These needs occur when the organisation decides that it has to adopt a major new strategy, create a new product or service, undergo a large-scale change programme, or develop significant new relationships, such as joining with others to form new partnerships.

The reason that so many major change programmes fail (over 75 per cent, according to various research studies) is that they do not recognise the need to take a holistic view of *all* the systems – technical, human, financial, and marketing – and they do not involve a wide range of stakeholders in designing and implementing the change. BICC cables, Manchester, already described in this chapter, is one example of a change at this level.

Another example of change at the innovating level is Rivelin Stainless Steel, which had been making significant losses for a number of years. It was then bought by another company and new senior managers were installed, who asked the trade union to take responsibility for redesigning production processes so that productivity would rise, costs would fall, and there would be no compulsory redundancies. Working together with management, the union achieved this seemingly impossible task and the company is now one of the most profitable in the world.

Group needs

These concern the performance of a particular group, which may be a team, department, function, subunit, or so on. Information about this group's performance may identify areas of need – which, again, may be for training or other interventions.

I_1: implementing level

In this case ITN is about finding out how efficiently a particular team or group goes about its business and meets its current objectives.

The design team in a small firm of consulting engineers employed three specialists – one in heating and ventilation, one in electrical installations, and one in plumbing and drainage. Unfortunately, although called a 'team', in no way did these three people work as such. Rather, each ignored the others and concentrated on his or her own specialism. As a result, the heating and ventilation specialist's design took up all the services space available, leaving none for the other two, who in turn (working individually) did the same sort of thing. The result was that designs had to be reworked, with additional cost and time penalties.

I_2: improving level

This level is where many continuous improvement projects are to be found, because these are usually carried out by teams. The team is able to identify improvement areas and also works together effectively to carry out many process and systems improvements.

Comparisons between Japanese and European car manufacturers show some of the benefits that can be partly attributed to teamworking at this level.

	European companies	Japanese companies
% of workforce in teams	0.6	69.3
Productivity-hours per car	36.2	16.8
Quality-defects per 100 vehicles	97.0	60.0

I_3: innovating
level

By working effectively with other teams across boundaries, major changes can be brought about, better relationships and communications be established, and new ways of working together be formed.

The BICC case already cited involved, as a key element, teams from different shifts talking and negotiating with one another about the handover arrangements.

Simply by talking with its internal customer, a data-processing department in a petrochemicals company discovered that a monthly report that took four days to produce, including working on a Sunday night, was not in fact required! What was wanted was a one-page summary that could have been produced by one person in less than an hour.

Yet again, comparing Japanese and European car manufacturers produces interesting results.

	European companies	Japanese companies
% of workforce in teams	0.6	69.3
Creativity: suggestions per employee	0.4	61.6
Engineering hours per 100 vehicles	3,000,000	1,700,000

Individual needs

These concern the performance of one or more individuals (*as* individuals, rather than as members of a group). Again this information may identify specific needs.

I_1: implementing level

Here ITN is about finding out to what extent individuals need to learn or be trained

- to bring their current performance up to the required level
- as a result of changes in methods and processes that call for new competencies and skills.

I_2: improving level

Here ITN is about looking at the extent to which individuals need to learn or be trained in systematic, continuous improvement skills and how to take initiatives.

I_3: innovating level

Finally, this is where we find out whether individuals need to learn how to think holistically, work across boundaries, examine their assumptions, or work with people from different backgrounds and with different perspectives.

In Table 3 (on page 24) individual, group, and organisational learning needs are brought together at each of the three levels of performance, showing the wide range of what we may need to consider when carrying out a thorough training-needs analysis.

Using the frameworks for ITN included in this introductory chapter it is possible to see the wide variety of training needs that might arise if we take a thorough, broadly-based approach. In later chapters we shall examine training needs in more detail under the headings organisational, group, and individual.

Table 3

ORGANISATIONAL, GROUP, AND INDIVIDUAL NEEDS AT THE THREE LEVELS OF PERFORMANCE

Area of need / Level of business benefit	Organisational	Group	Individual
I_1: Implementing – doing things well	Meeting current organisational objectives	Working together to meet existing targets and standards	Being competent at the level of existing requirements
I_2: Improving – doing things better	Setting higher objectives and reaching them	Continuous improvement teams	Having and using systematic, continuous improvement skills and processes
I_3: Innovating – doing new and better things	Changing objectives and strategies	Working across boundaries to create new relationships and new products and services	Being able to work differently and more creatively with a shared sense of purpose

In brief

In this chapter we have tried to lay down some groundrules for ITN against which we shall measure its effectiveness and usefulness in subsequent chapters. To enable us to make this continuous assessment of ITN we have provided a framework of organisational, group, and individual performance which is a common starting-point for all ITN activities. We are making the assumption that ITN is really about delivering effective training, learning, and development, and that the purpose of training is to enhance performance through learning. More specifically we can say that

∎ training needs have to be related to business aims and objectives

∎ we require ways of integrating training needs with business outcomes and benefits

∎ the framework for making such integration that has been introduced here establishes that there are three different levels of performance for meeting the full range of organisational objectives:

Doing things well	– I_1 Implementing
Doing things better	– I_2 Improving
Doing new and better things	– I_3 Innovating

You should now be in a position to examine your own organisation's objectives and performance needs in these terms.

We have also discovered that different methods of learning and training are required for performance at the three levels. These can be summarised as:

Mode 1 – Adhering

Mode 2 – Adapting

Mode 3 – Relating

Mode 4 – Experiencing

Mode 5 – Experimenting

Mode 6 – Connecting

Mode 7 – Dedicating

We hope that this framework will enable you to identify more clearly and precisely your organisation's needs for learning and training. Finally, to help you locate where very general needs might exist, we have added a further framework, because we have found it useful to recognise that performance and needs for learning and training can also be considered from the point of view of the organisation as a whole, or of teams and groups, or of individuals. On this basis we shall now examine the processes of ITN in more detail.

Reference

PEDLER MJ, BURGOYNE JG and BOYDELL TH *The Learning Company*. Maidenhead; McGraw-Hill, 2nd edition, 1996.

2

Obtaining Information for ITN

Although there are numerous techniques for collecting, analysing and presenting data – many of which are described in later chapters – it is useful to consider two main sets of information that can help us to identify training needs. These are:

- information about current performance
- information about future changes.

We shall look at both of these in turn.

Information about current performance

There are three main ways of obtaining data about current performance:

- using objective data
- getting feedback from others
- using self-assessment.

We shall now describe these three, because we shall be using them in later chapters.

Using objective data

Perhaps this heading should be 'allegedly objective data'! It can be argued that no data is or can be truly objective. However, when we use the phrase in this book we are referring to such quantified data about performance as output, productivity, delivery times, and so on.

What sort of data do we have in mind? Really, the list is endless. Here are just some variables that could be used:

Productivity   Output in units per hour/day/week etc.

Output in units per employee.

Output in units per square foot.

Output in value as a ratio to capital employed.

Time to carry out a specific task, to provide service, to produce goods.

Machine down-time.

Quality or delivery of product/service   Length of waiting-lists (numbers of customers).

Time that customers have to wait.

Percentage of on-time deliveries.

Defects per unit of production.

Errors in providing service.

Complaints per number of customers served.

Commendations per number of customers served.

Wasted staff hours.

Time spent on rework.

Scrap/wastage – as percentage of units produced
– as percentage of raw materials used
– cash value
– cash value as percentage of turnover.

Financial/ commercial   Turnover.

Profit.

Cost per unit of production.

Cost per customer served.

Return on capital.

Share price.

Dividends.

Value of debtors.

Length of time debts have been outstanding.

Cash flow; overdraft management.

Market share.

Personnel   Accident rate.

Sickness and absenteeism.

Staff turnover

Percentage of staff employed on short-term contract or agency basis.

Percentage with competencies or qualifications (eg NVQs).

Age/gender/race profiles.

Number of unfilled vacancies.

Length of service.

Percentage who receive appraisals.

Intellectual capital.

Environment   Waste discharge and pollution levels (solids, liquids, gases).

Noise levels.

Light pollution levels.

Environmental Load Units.

> Which of the above types of data are currently used in your organisation?
>
> Which could be used but are not?
>
> Can you think of others that are used or could be used?

The data to use will be that which is relevant to that aspect of the individual, group, or organisation that you are investigating, and (by definition) those which are available! The latter point may sound obvious, but very often you cannot obtain the sort of data you might want to use, or it is not available in an accessible or usable form. It may never have been collected, or, if collected, kept for only a short time, or again, only in aggregated form – not broken down by groups or individuals.

An early task in setting up an ITN process might therefore be to identify the data that would be helpful, to check to see whether it is available and, if not, to set up a system for collecting the data from that time on. Data of this nature is useless on its own. To be of value, it has to be compared with something – for example, with:

■ figures for *other* individuals, groups, or organisations

■ past figures for the *same* individual, group, or organisation

■ a target or objective.

Making such comparisons is not as straightforward as is often assumed. Failure to recognise this may very well lead to interventions – training or otherwise – that, at best, waste time but, at worst, may actually create more problems! (Further guidance on making these comparisons is given in Chapter 4.)

Getting feedback from others

Feedback from others is a very common approach for obtaining information. Although this may, of course, include objective data of the type explored earlier in this chapter, very often it is more subjective, involving qualitative information such as opinions and rating scales. For a brief overview we shall list typical methods (explained in more detail in Chapter 8).

Feedback from others to individuals about their performance may involve competency frameworks, appraisal, or 360° feedback.

Feedback from others to groups about their performance may involve customer-mapping, role negotiation, or a functional audit.

Feedback from
others to
organisations   about their performance may involve customer surveys, benchmarking, or an environmental audit.

Using self-assessment

As well as obtaining data from others, it is often helpful to think about oneself and in so doing to use a structured method of providing one's own feedback.

At the individual
level   this may involve a number of processes. (See another title in the Training Essentials series, *Cultivating Self-Development*, D Megginson and V Whitaker, IPD, 1996.) In this book we shall show how you can use either open-ended incident analysis or a framework of competencies to assess yourself. (See Chapter 9.)

At the group
level   members may, for example, rate themselves and one another on group skills or on the stage of development of the group as a whole. (See Chapter 8.)

At the
organisational
level   feedback from oneself primarily involves looking at such issues as mission, vision, values, and strategy. (See Chapter 7.) Internal surveys might also be seen as falling into this category, although we are treating them as feedback from others.

Information about future changes

As well as shortfalls in current performance, future changes will usually give rise to a number of needs, including some for training or retraining.

What sorts of changes do we have in mind? Well, quite a number, in fact!

Changes in market/client base

One obvious set of changes concerns market conditions. Some organisations are faced with growing markets whilst others are shrinking; often it is a question of increased competition either locally or, not unusually these days, from overseas. In the non-commercial sector, too, the client base may well be changing. Furthermore, with various privatisations, 'market-testing', and the like, many public-sector organisations find themselves in competition with private-sector firms or with newly formed government agencies.

To survive, let alone flourish, under these conditions our organisations will have to learn. Learning to implement (I_1) will no longer be sufficient: they will have to learn to do things better than their competitors (I_2), which, as we have seen in Chapter 1, involves people learning to operate in modes 4 and 5.

The voluntary sector is similarly faced with competition from other agencies' coming onto the scene. Another form of competition in this sector is that for scarce funds – thrown into sharp relief by the advent of the National Lottery, which has by all accounts drained large sums of money away from many charities. Complex inter-agency working – eg between schools, the police, and social services – calls for new skills. In particular, it requires abilities at level I_3 (innovating). Organisations faced with these types of change need to learn to do new and better things together – they need to learn to work in modes 6 and 7. The same applies in the commercial sector, where changes in market, costs of development projects, and the scope and complexity of national or international projects all require a high level of ability to form partnerships and to work together creatively.

Recent research by multinational consultants A T Kearney, has shown, for example, that companies that go into partnerships because they are more or less forced to by market conditions tend to stress the importance of setting up procedures and rules for working together, and then of learning to stick to these rules. Their emphasis is on I_1 (implementing). By contrast, organisations that go into partnering agreements because they see these as opportunities for creativity and innovation are more likely to recognise the importance of putting effort, time, and other resources into learning to work together, to see whole pictures, and to recognise, value, and gain benefit from the diversity that each side brings to the partnership. They are learning to work at level I_3 (innovating).

Changes in technology

Often linked with market changes, changes in technology will give rise to learning and training needs. To start with, people will need to learn to operate new equipment properly, learning at level I_1 (implementing).

Some technology is so complex, however, and involves so much for customers and users to get the most of it, that people will need to learn once again to work together creatively at level I_3 (innovating). A familiar example of this is information technology (IT), where all sorts of things are technically possible but where actual users of systems are often left out of the picture at the design and development stages. Technical experts are great at design and improvement but are unable to put themselves in the position of the users – they cannot see things from their perspective. The result of this inability to learn to work together is that users get frustrated when they cannot make the systems work, and end up seeing IT people as unhelpful. At the same time IT people see users as old-fashioned, ungrateful, or downright stupid! For organisations the cost in delays, errors, and rework is huge.

Changes in legislation or standards

Obviously, numerous legislative changes can affect an organisation, be they in the fields of employment, health and safety, environmental protection, trade, taxation, or whatever. People will need to learn the new legislation to know what is required, and may well need creative solutions to be able to comply with it. For example, if lower pollution levels are called for, then our ways of working and our use of equipment and raw materials may need to be changed.

A similar situation applies to standards – which are not so much a legal requirement as standards that customers, say, will be looking for. An obvious example is ISO 9000, the quality standard; many customers will deal with only those suppliers who have been awarded it. Some organisations set out to go beyond the basic standard and, for example, seek to win the European Quality Award, which gives an indication to others that they are something special. Another standard with clear implications for training needs is Investors In People (IIP), awarded through Training and Enterprise Councils to organisations that meet specified requirements for the planning, organisation, and implementation of training programmes. (See the Appendix for more on IIPs.)

Reorganisations and other internal initiatives

Often an organisation's response to changing circumstances is to reorganise, perhaps in conjunction with a major internal change programme such as teamworking, customer care, total quality, process re-engineering, or whatever its chosen developmental strategy may be. Changes of this magnitude are, of course, going to reveal major learning needs – particularly in level I_3 (innovating) and learning to work together.

Finding out more about changes

Once you have recognised future changes and their broad implications, you will need to find out much more. A useful way to do this is to identify all the people and processes likely to be affected by the change, and then learn more about exactly how they will be affected, by talking with the various stakeholders, probing, attending meetings and so on.

What changes are facing you and your organisation in each of the areas listed below?

What are your first thoughts about the implications for training needs?

How can you explore these further?

Market/client base

Technology

Legislation or standards

Reorganisation/other internal initiatives

Giving and receiving feedback
Higher and lower self

Giving and receiving feedback on current performance or the implications of future changes usually involves emotions. It addresses areas of insecurity and anxiety, as well as raising possibilities for positive development. It is therefore important to think about this aspect of the process, and the model of 'higher and lower self' is a useful starting-point.

The idea of 'higher and lower selves' was originally used

in the context of individual feedback and development (Boydell 1985). At that level, the higher self may be said to be the part of you that represents your good qualities – the part that may be honest, courageous, kind, open-minded, and so on. Conversely, the lower self, or the shadow side, contains less worthy characteristics, such as insecurity, pride, greed, envy, and selfishness.

> ▮ Can you identify some of the aspects of your higher self?
>
> ▮ Under what circumstances do these shine through?
>
> ▮ Are they likely to be seen in particular types of situation, in response to specific challenges, when working with certain people?
>
> ▮ What are the consequences?
>
> ▮ Similarly, what of your lower self: what is this made up of?
>
> ▮ What brings into play this aspect of you – what situations, circumstances, challenges, or people?
>
> ▮ What are the consequences?

Just as each individual may be said to have a higher and lower self, so do groups and organisations (and perhaps even societies). Certain collective positive and negative features can be associated with a group or an organisation.

> Think of a group of which you are a member: can you identify aspects of its higher and lower selves; what triggers these aspects off; what the consequences are?
>
> Now what about your organisation as a whole?

The way we – as individuals, a group or an organisation – receive feedback is very much affected by the extent to which we do so through our higher or lower self, as shown in Figures 4 and 5 (on pages 38–9). First, when your lower self takes charge (Figure 4), even positive feedback becomes distorted and channelled in a way that stops it being helpful. Complacency, self-satisfaction, and pride result from a perception of your own brilliance (or that of your group, or indeed of your organisation as a whole) and prevent you from working on any of your weaknesses. But 'pride comes before a fall' – after which it is too late.

> IBM is a case in point. For many years a feature of its lower self was a degree of pride and arrogance that in effect cut it off from looking at what was going on in the market. Hence, when competitors created the demand for PCs rather than mainframe computers IBM got into a real mess:
>
>> The company simply missed the potential of laptops, a mistake even less easy to explain than the original lag in PCs... The mistake showed extraordinary myopia – and arrogance – for a market leader.
>
>> Heller (1994)

When the lower self is in charge, negative feedback is also misused. After all, if you are receiving some information about negative aspects of yourself or your performance, then this, although unpleasant, does at least represent an opportunity for improvement. In the hands of the lower self, however, this opportunity is lost. Instead of being considered objectively, the negative information triggers off insecurities and denials, usually followed almost immediately by all sorts of other negative, aggressive, and hostile responses, including sarcasm, resentment, annoyance, grumbling, brooding, spite, rage, and bitterness. Usually these are directed at the source of discomfort – ie the person responsible for the feedback – although other innocent bystanders often become the target! At other times it is yourself whom you take aim at, and you engage

Figure 4
FEEDBACK INFORMATION RECEIVED BY THE LOWER SELF

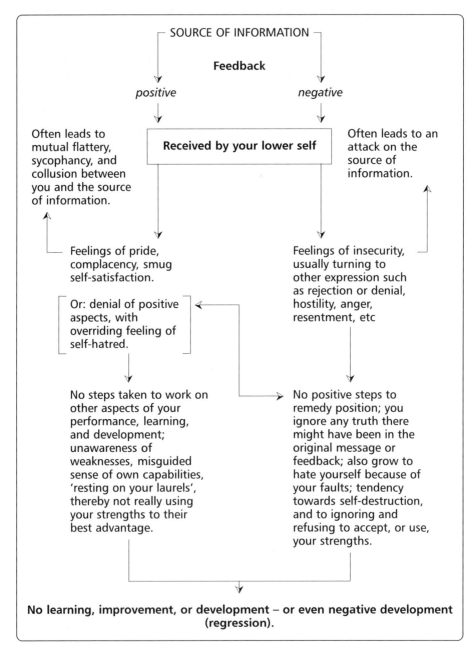

Figure 5

FEEDBACK INFORMATION RECEIVED BY THE HIGHER SELF

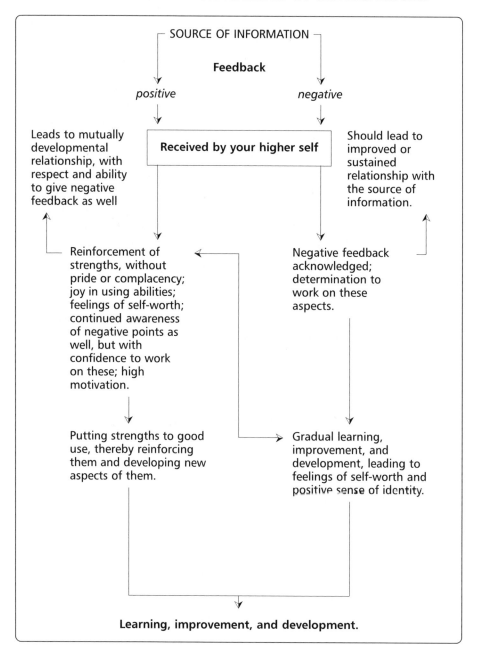

SOURCE OF INFORMATION

Feedback

positive   *negative*

Leads to mutually developmental relationship, with respect and ability to give negative feedback as well

Received by your higher self

Should lead to improved or sustained relationship with the source of information.

Reinforcement of strengths, without pride or complacency; joy in using abilities; feelings of self-worth; continued awareness of negative points as well, but with confidence to work on these; high motivation.

Negative feedback acknowledged; determination to work on these aspects.

Putting strengths to good use, thereby reinforcing them and developing new aspects of them.

Gradual learning, improvement, and development, leading to feelings of self-worth and positive sense of identity.

Learning, improvement, and development.

in moods of self-destruction – or even self-destructive acts, such as becoming accident-prone, developing stress diseases, taking foolishly dangerous risks, attacking fellow group members, becoming addicted to tobacco, alcohol, or drugs, or overworking. This is hardly the route to learning and improvement.

Compare this with feedback received by your higher self (Figure 5). In this case, negative feedback, although unpleasant, really is seen as an opportunity for development. With determination and courage, you resolve to do something – to work on improving your performance and yourself. At the same time, positive feedback is received and acknowledged, adding to your non-complacent, prideless feelings of self-worth and leading to a positive sense of identity: 'It is all right to be me.' There is a further bonus: the very act of responding with your higher self is a way of recognising it, of getting in touch with it. This in itself enhances learning and development.

In fact, one's *initial* reaction to negative feedback very often engages with the lower self. A well-known formulation is illustrated in Figure 6. At point ① the initial

Figure 6

HOW NEGATIVE FEEDBACK IS MANAGED OVER TIME

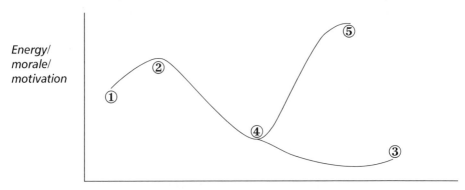

feedback is often denied. This is then followed by anger against the source of the information ② – which raises energy levels, although not in a particularly constructive way! Once the anger passes, feelings become increasingly depressed. Somewhere along this part of the curve (between ② and ③) apathy may set in more or less permanently. More positively, however, a trough may be reached and some form of facing-up to the situation takes place ④. This is where your higher self takes charge and gets you back on the 'learning curve' ⑤.

> Think of a time when you received some negative feedback.
> Then draw *your* chart, plotting energy up the vertical axis and time along the horizontal. Where did you end up? What was there about the situation (what happened, the people involved) that influenced how you responded?
>
> Can you do the same for a group you have been in, where overall group morale was affected by feedback?

ITN very much involves giving feedback. Therefore when doing so – by writing a report, oral presentation, or whatever – keep the following questions in mind (these have been written from the point of view of someone giving feedback to an individual, but the same questions will be helpful when working with a group):

▌ Is what I want to say a combination of positive and negative feedback? If so, it is generally accepted that it is much better to start with the positive, because this strengthens the other person's self-image, making it very much easier for him or her to hear and work with the negative when you come to give that.

▌ How is the other person responding to this feedback? How does he or she appear to be feeling? What does he or she want to do as a result? (If I don't know the answer to these questions, how might I find out?)

- How am *I* feeling in this situation? What do I want to do?
- As the person giving the feedback, where are my higher and lower selves? What is my motive – to be helpful? Or to score points? Or to punish? Or to sell my favourite, packaged solution?
- Am I presenting the information in an appropriate way? Is it clear? Am I giving it in a way that shows that we have possible solutions in mind? (Concentrate on behaviour and solutions, not on labelling somebody. For example, 'You seem to be having problems with spelling; do you think that it would help if we installed a spell-checker and showed you how to use it?' [behaviour and possible solution] is much easier to handle than 'You are a poor speller' [personal labelling].)
- What am I doing to help the other person handle and manage their feelings? For example, you might simply ask how they feel. Or say how *you* would feel in these circumstances.

In brief

We have now established a rule of thumb about ITN: the quality (not necessarily the quantity) of information upon which we base our ITN analysis will go a long way to determining how useful and accurate the whole exercise will have been. It is a variation on the old computer slogan: 'GIGO – Garbage In, Garbage Out'. In this case, QIQO – Quality In, Quality Out.

We find, however, that we must be imaginative and creative in obtaining information, as well as systematic, logical, and thorough. In this chapter we have deliberately introduced approaches to obtaining information that stretch the boundaries of traditional practice in this area. It could well be that if we widen our perspective and look for information in unlikely places we shall make some important new discoveries. In fact, this is a rather important theme we have introduced here, and one that we shall work on in later chapters. Here we have been concerned with learning about different ways of obtaining information – about current performance and future changes. The main points we have covered are these:

∎ In obtaining information about current performance, it is important to use objective data wherever possible, but it is not always the case that quantified data is the only type we need to examine. It tells only part of the story.

∎ We must therefore also look at somewhat more objective data, such as that we obtain when we get feedback from others. This kind of information can be about other individuals, groups, or the organisation as a whole.

∎ Information about current performance can come from oneself, using a structured method.

∎ Information about future changes is often the trigger for directing training effort towards identified needs. Here we have looked at changes in markets (linked to our performance/learning model); changes in technology; in legislation or standards; reorganisations and other internal initiatives.

∎ Finally in this chapter, we have introduced an important way of handling information: giving and receiving feedback from the point of view of higher and lower selves.

References

BOYDELL TH *Management Self-Development*. Geneva; International Labour Office, 1985.

HELLER R *The Fate of IBM*. London; Little, Brown & Co., 1994.

MEGGINSON D and WHITAKER V *Cultivating Self-Development*. London; IPD, 1996.

Roles, Relationships and Skills in ITN

In this chapter we shall look at some of the human factors involved in ITN: roles, relationships, and skills.

Who is involved?

Primary and secondary roles

Those with primary roles in an ITN exercise are the people (individuals or groups) whose needs are being identified. So here we are talking about 'my needs', 'our needs' – to which a high degree of ownership can be attached. A secondary role is played by those who provide information or feedback and various forms of assistance, expertise, and support. These people are concerned with 'other people's needs' and therefore the commitment to ITN is different – less personal and more professional perhaps. There may also be a different set of motives at work here, such as providing a service, assisting others to improve their performance, carrying out a functional role (HR/training staff), providing resources, making decisions, or interpreting information.

The learners or trainees involved in the ITN process may participate directly themselves or work through some kind of representation system, such as trade unions, informal spokespeople, or focus groups. The latter are made up of people who in some sense reflect the system as a whole. For example, rather than working with all members of the workforce, a group of, say, 10 people may be chosen, either at random, by asking for volunteers, or by getting nominations, to speak on their behalf.

In answer to the question, 'Who is likely to be involved in ITN?', we may find some or all of the people mentioned in Figure 7.

Figure 7

PEOPLE INVOLVED IN ITN

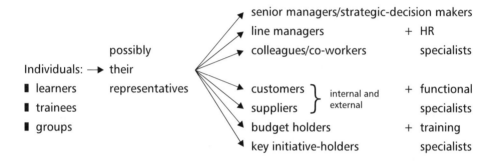

How are people involved?
Learners

Learners are those who may have a training need and should be involved whenever possible. This may sound obvious, but surprisingly enough they are often left out! Indeed, one of the basic beliefs of the 'systematic training' of the 1970s was that external experts were to decide what others needed to learn.

There are a number of reasons for involving learners. To start with, they hold much information about what is going on. They can help analyse the situation and decide what needs changing – including, possibly, training for themselves – using techniques like the 'fishbone' (Chapter 5). Another reason for involving learners is that by so doing you are likely to get a much higher level of commitment to any programmes or changes.

In BICC the teamleaders were invited to identify areas in which they would like further training. This they did, meeting in groups to shape up a list of competencies that they wanted to acquire. The final result was not much different from what could have been acquired 'off the shelf', but the *process* of involving them meant that they felt involved, were highly motivated, and were in fact practising working together and thinking systematically about themselves, what they were doing, and why they were doing it (modes 5 to 7 – levels I_2 (Improving) and I_3 (Innovating) – as described in Chapter 1).

Colleagues and co-workers

These can often provide valuable information either informally or through systematic processes such as 360° feedback involving co-workers, bosses, subordinates, customers and suppliers. (See Chapter 9.)

Line managers

These need to take part in various ways. Of course, they may well be a source of information, providing either objective data or feedback that is more subjective. Line managers also play a key part in encouraging individuals and in creating the right conditions and resources for them to receive feedback and engage in subsequent learning activities.

Senior managers/strategic-decision-makers

Such people, of course, provide the overall direction, mission, vision, strategy, and so on within which ITN is being carried out. It can be argued that, without these, any ITN exercise will be lacking any real purpose. (Chapter 7 describes a number of ways of exploring this area.)

A local authority in the west of England was running a programme for supervisors. They were asked to take part in identifying their own learning needs. In reply, the supervisors – encouraged by the training manager – told their line managers that they could not do this until they had more information about where the authority was going. What were the mission, vision, and strategy over the next five years to be, and how would this affect their role, and hence their learning needs?

In fact their line managers could not answer these questions, and so held meetings with senior managers to find out. This in turn forced the senior managers to become much clearer about these issues, as a result of which they engaged in an extensive exercise of consulting the local population, as well as staff at all levels.

In this case, therefore, a question about level I_1 (implementing) needs led to a level I_3 (innovating) enquiry process.

Clients and customers

As will be seen in the local authority example, *clients and customers* may often be the source of data, again producing either objective figures or relatively subjective opinions. At the organisational level, (internal or external) customer surveys are often used, either on their own or in conjunction with focus groups or 'customer panels'. (See Chapter 6.)

One of the major gains in the field of quality improvement has been the recognition that, just as the organisation as a whole has external customers, each department, team, or indeed individual also has their own internal customers. Various processes such as customer-mapping, role negotiation, and functional audit and 360° feedback may be used for obtaining information at group or individual levels. (See Chapters 8 and 9.)

Suppliers

In practice, *suppliers* tend to be much less involved in ITN, although in our view they can play a key part. People often treat suppliers, internal or external, very badly, which in the long run causes problems not only for the suppliers but also for the clients.

> A printing company obtained a contract from a rose-growing nursery to design and produce a catalogue. Time and again the client kept changing the specifications – catalogue size, number of pages, weight of paper, proportion of products to be illustrated by colour pictures, actual pictures to be used – which made the printer's job very difficult. The nursery thought they were being creative and flexible. But the supplier could have told them quite a lot about the need to have a good internal procedure for formulating the specification and then sticking to it.

Suppliers, therefore, should be involved in ways similar to customers.

Budget holders

Be they line managers or holders of specialist funds, these people need to be involved, because without their support you will probably be unable to do anything about the needs that you identify.

Key-initiative takers

This category includes people in charge of particular projects or programmes, such as Investors In People (see the Appendix), quality, business process re-engineering, customer care, and so on. They may well be the initiators of a process of identifying training needs. Alternatively you may be able to get their support and hitch your training-wagon to their star, to paraphrase a metaphor!

Specialists

Finally, any number of *functional specialists*, not least HR or training specialists, will of course have a stake in any ITN process that you may be carrying out, and will therefore want to be involved in various ways.

We suggest that you use the above as a check-list. For any particular ITN exercise, identify the people (by name, wherever possible), think through their possible involvement, and then go and talk to them. Table 4 (on page 50) suggests a pro forma for doing this, although you can of course design your own or simply write down your ideas on a sheet of paper.

Political influences

It would be naive to assume that ITN is a neutral, disinterested exercise. The politics of the situation form a vital ingredient and have to be managed carefully. It may not be usual to use a 'hard' word such as 'political' to describe one of the various influences on ITN, but we feel it is appropriate. People have a stake in the outcome of ITN and therefore wish to exert their influence. They may wish to ensure that the exercise is conducted in a particular way (eg to involve certain people); they may hope for certain outcomes which they will try to influence; decisions have to be made regarding costs, budgets, and investments; priorities have to be chosen, and it may not be possible to satisfy everyone.

It is true for most of us that as soon as the subject of ITN is raised then we tend to assume that these needs *will* be satisfied in some way or other. Yet it may not be possible to do this. There is no shortage of needs in most situations – but the means of satisfying them may be limited. Raising people's expectations and then not being able to satisfy them may leave a feeling of disappointment. Indeed, whenever choices have to be made between the demands and requirements of one group and another, the possibility

ITN Exercise *Stakeholders*	What will they want from the exercise?	What can they contribute to the exercise?	What help do I need from them?	What help can I give them?	Comments
Learners (individuals; teams/groups; or organisation as a whole):					
Colleagues and co-workers:					
Line managers:					
Senior managers/strategic-decision-makers:					
Clients/customers (internal/external):					
Suppliers (internal/external):					
Budget holders:					
Key-initiative takers:					
Functional specialists:					
HR/training specialists:					

Table 4

PEOPLE INVOLVED IN ITN

of disenchantment arises. Some people and groups within the political system of the organisation will have more power and influence than others. Are the most powerful always going to get their way? How can we perhaps equalise this power? It is not inevitable that the powerful get their way: in recent years groups who in the past have been relatively disadvantaged, such as women and ethnic minorities, have been given more opportunities to have their needs identified and met through affirmative action and equal opportunities.

It may be worthwhile identifying some of the political influences in your ITN situation; you can use the 'map' in Figure 8 (on page 52) as a guide. You can then decide how you might best take account of these various influences.

In examining and taking account of these political issues, those involved have to face difficult questions and to find a way of dealing with them. Typical questions include:

- How is the ITN exercise likely to be carried out?
- What range of training opportunities are we prepared to provide to meet the needs identified?
- Who decides on priorities?
- Who is to get priority?
- What do we do about those whose needs are not likely to be met?

Some of the prioritising techniques described later in this book (especially those in Chapter 5) may fruitfully be used here. Handling some of these issues may be a delicate and tricky business, for those who are disclosing information about training needs risk being labelled troublemakers.

Anyone carrying out an ITN exercise would do well to consider these and other political factors, and work out their own strategy for dealing with them. Each situation will undoubtedly be different, with its own set of constraints and influences at work. No easy or standard

Figure 8

SOME INFLUENCES ON THE IDENTIFICATION OF TRAINING NEEDS

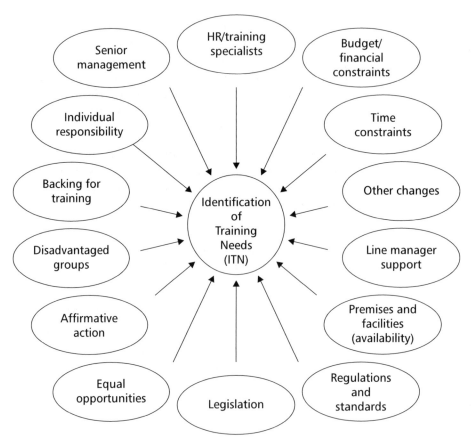

solution is possible, but it is always useful to know what you are likely to be up against – and who is on your side!

Among the commoner barriers you are likely to meet are:

▌ different learning styles and preferences. People learn in different ways and generally have some idea of what works best for them. This should be taken into account when identifying their training needs.

▌ attitudes to training. These vary according to people's

previous experience and, perhaps, the training culture of the organisation.

- ∎ 'training is punishment'. Training is seen as a remedial activity for those whose performance is seen as 'below par' or 'not up to scratch'. If this is a predominant attitude in the organisation, then people will be reluctant to admit to a need for training, because this implies there is something wrong with them. A more developmental approach is needed.

- ∎ 'training is a prize'. Training can be seen as a reward reserved for certain people. If a reward is on offer, people will be overanxious to have their need for this training identified, even if they do not really need it.

- ∎ 'ITN is a job for experts' (normally training or HR professionals). The assumption here is that only they should be involved.

- ∎ 'only managers know what is going on in the organisation'. Similarly, here the assumption is that only they know their staff, so all training and HR experts should be kept out.

- ∎ senior management see training as necessary for others – but not them. Suggesting that they too may need training might not be acceptable, and has to be handled differently – ie with great tact and care!

- ∎ 'only senior management know enough about what is going on to be able to appreciate what the organisation needs'. If this really were true, how come many people in the organisation (and outside) seem to have a more accurate picture of what is actually happening? Indeed there is a rule of thumb that says that the 'lower' you go in the organisation, the greater the understanding of what is needed!

Who identifies training needs?

Traditionally, training needs were identified by someone – usually from the training department – who acted in effect as a *'needs investigator'*. They sought data, analysed and interpreted it, and then came to conclusions about needs. A simple diagram illustrates this:

Training dept/HR ⟶ identifies learner's needs

This style remains quite common. However, nowadays a number of others are often found. For example, the *data-provider* style involves obtaining information, analysing it, and then feeding it back to the 'learners' (individual, group, or even whole organisation) for the latter to interpret themselves and come to their own conclusions. So the diagram now looks like this:

Training dept/HR ⟶ provides and ⟶ learners interpret
analyses data   data analysis to
determine own needs

Another variation is the *facilitator*, who helps learners to think of their own ways of collecting, analysing, and interpreting data, as well as coming to their own conclusions:

Training dept/HR ⟶ facilitates learners in collecting, analysing, and interpreting data for themselves

Given that, increasingly, trainers and HR staff are becoming internal consultants who help to create learning organisations, we very much see a shift towards these last two roles. Increasingly, too, they are being played by line managers as well as by people from training or HR, whose role may now be to help the line manager. Thus we may have something like this:

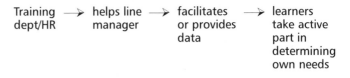

Training ⟶ helps line ⟶ facilitates ⟶ learners
dept/HR   manager   or provides   take active
data   part in
determining
own needs

> What role and style do you want to adopt when identifying training needs?
>
> Why?
>
> What alternatives have you considered?

The skills involved in ITN

So far we have looked at roles and influences in ITN. Now we can explore some of the skills involved. A good way of presenting these is by looking at them in three sets:

Process skills — setting goals, making plans, reviewing and evaluating the ITN process.

Relationship skills — building and maintaining a helpful relationship with the person or group whose needs are being identified

Content skills — getting information and analysing and making sense of it.

Process skills

Process skills are about setting goals, making plans, and deciding how you are going to carry out the ITN process. In effect they include thinking about the scope, purpose, and time-scale of the exercise, deciding whom to involve, and how. You will need to think about getting together other resources, including facilities (eg computing) for analysing your information once you have collected it. You will also have to decide on your feedback strategy. Will this be by means of a written report, or orally, or some combination? How much will the exercise cost? Do you hold the budget for this? If not, can you acquire it?

Once you have got the ITN exercise under way, you will need to review it. How well is it going? How do you know? How can you find out? Are you on track with the project, or do you need to change your plans or reschedule your timetable?

Relationship skills

We have already described some of the roles – and politics – in ITN. It is clear, therefore, that ITN is very much a social process, ie it involves a number of interpersonal relationships. These will be between various individuals (eg trainer, line manager, learner, senior manager); within groups (ie between group members); and between groups (eg those in other departments, units, teams, professions, or trades). What are the skills required for making these relationships work well? In broad terms we can summarise these into two clusters: supporting, and confronting.

Obviously, ITN often involves *supporting skills* such as listening and showing empathy (ie showing that you deeply understand how others are feeling). Whether it be in obtaining information, feeding it back, or helping someone to make sense of it, supportive skills will be required.

At times, however, you will need to be *confronting* or challenging. If someone is denying the validity of feedback, you may well have to stick to your guns, be assertive and insist (albeit in a friendly way) that he or she listens to what you are saying and considers its possible merits. You will also, at times, need to be confronting and assertive in order to take initiatives and obtain information that others may prefer you not to have. Confronting can also be useful when helping someone to derive meaning from the information you have supplied. There may be a danger of 'rationalisation', of explaining things away. If this happens, you may well need to point it out.

Content skills

Content skills are, first, to do with deciding what information to collect, finding sources, and obtaining and recording the information. In general we can refer to this as *collecting data*. Much of this book is about ways of doing this. It is, of course, important not to get bogged down in too much detail. This is where you will have to use your judgement: is more information needed, or will it get in the way?

You may often find it helpful to be able to give examples to illustrate your findings and back up your conclusions. This may be in the form of objective data, or, by contrast, stories and incidents. Similarly, if someone is talking to you about problems or needs that he or she sees in the organisation, it will help if you ask that person for examples.

Once the information has been collected, it needs to be analysed for patterns, trends, implications, and overviews, and to be summarised. Although still about 'content', these processes – which for simplicity we shall call *analysing data* – are quite different from *collecting data*. The latter involves a lot of detail, whereas the purpose of analysis is to look behind the detail and recognise the underlying pattern, essence, theme, or meaning that is there, and then to summarise this. When interpreting data, you need to be very aware of your own assumptions, prejudices, and stereotypes. Keep open-minded, and watch out for the danger of imposing your own preferred meanings on the situation.

When talking with others about interpretations and meanings, look out for rationalisations, either by the other person(s) or indeed by yourself! Rationalising or dismissing some difficult information by explaining it away, or blaming someone else or some apparently random factor (such as the weather!), is often used as a defence mechanism. (Chapter 5 provides some useful tools to help with analysis.)

The 'star cluster' of skills involved

You will have noticed that each of the three groups of skills – process, relationship and content – consists of two main clusters, which in a way complement one another. So we have:

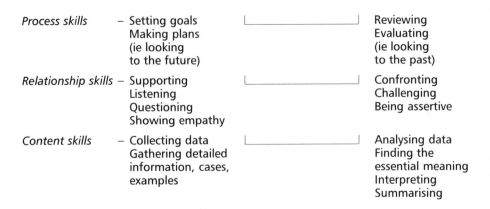

Process skills — Setting goals
Making plans
(ie looking
to the future)

Reviewing
Evaluating
(ie looking
to the past)

Relationship skills — Supporting
Listening
Questioning
Showing empathy

Confronting
Challenging
Being assertive

Content skills — Collecting data
Gathering detailed
information, cases,
examples

Analysing data
Finding the
essential meaning
Interpreting
Summarising

We find it helpful to draw these three dimensions in a way that makes a 'star-shape', as in Figure 9. What happens at the centre of the star? That is where you find the ability

Figure 9

THE SKILLS 'STAR CLUSTER'

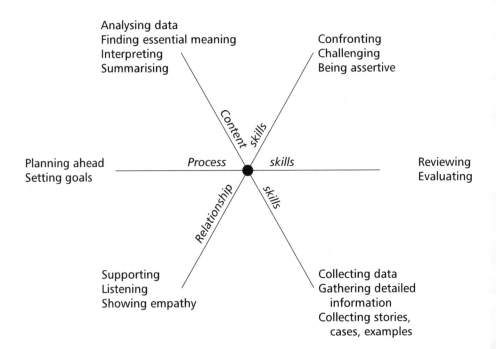

to step back, look at what you are doing, and become aware of your own assumptions, prejudices, stereotypes, and feelings – about the ITN exercise, the data, or the people involved. This central skill is also about knowing when it is appropriate to bring in each of the others.

So you need to be able to decide when you have done enough planning and it is time to get some data – or when to stop collecting data (enough is enough) and start to analyse it. Conversely, there may be times when you realise that you do not yet have enough information; perhaps you need some examples to illustrate your findings, so you will have to go and collect them. Similarly with the relationship dimension; you have to decide when to be supportive and when to challenge or confront – and how to do the latter in a way that is in fact not seen as a direct attack! So all the time you are carrying out your ITN exercise you need to keep an overview of all these skills, call upon them when required, and balance them with one another.

In brief

In this chapter we have concentrated on the people involved in ITN – their roles, responsibilities and possible contributions. In reflecting on people's roles we (meaning the writers as well as the readers) have made some important learning discoveries, even if only to re-emphasise how vital people's enthusiasm, commitment, and dedication are in carrying out a successful ITN exercise. Everyone is dependent on one another for success – which indicates what an important developmental experience ITN can be for all those involved. Among the most significant learning points are those concerned with:

■ recognising the importance of secondary as well as primary roles in ITN.

■ seeing that people's perceptions and experiences of ITN will be different depending on whether they are identifying 'my' needs or 'their' needs. This brings up the question of ownership and involvement in the ITN process.

■ identifying the wide range of people who will be involved in an ITN exercise, each with their different contribution to make, including the learners themselves; managers; clients and customers; suppliers (maybe); others we may not immediately think of, such as budget holders, and initiative takers; and functional specialists and training professionals.

■ examining the many 'political' influences concerned with ITN – especially concerning those individuals who possess little power themselves but need someone to represent their interests, such as the disadvantaged or disenchanted. This may mean there is still a place for the 'welfare' and representative role for trainers and HR professionals.

■ seeing how pressure groups and interested parties exert their influence, make their needs and requirements known, and express various aspirations, values, and priorities. Anyone carrying out an ITN exercise needs to consider these factors carefully and work out their own strategy for dealing with them.

■ the blocks and barriers likely to be faced – recognising them, coming to terms with them and working out ways of dealing with them.

■ different overall roles within ITN under the headings of 'needs investigator', 'data provider' and 'facilitator'. You will now be able to make a more informed choice about which role you need to play (and how to get others involved to make their contribution).

■ the 'star cluster' of skills and how these can be applied to enhance the ITN process, making it as developmental an experience as possible for all concerned. We now have a better idea of where, when and how to apply particular skill clusters, using process, relationship, and content skills appropriately, sensitively, and effectively.

4

Comparing Data

We saw in Chapter 2 that one important source of information for ITN is 'objective data', which is usually numerical, quantitative. Subjective data, too, is often quantified, for example by using a range of rating scales, feedback scores, and so on, as will be described in later chapters. Whenever we are using quantitative data for analysis, presentation, and interpretation we need to look into it further to see what it is telling us. To do this we need to *compare* it with something.

Comparison of data

You have to have some target, norm, or standard to compare quantitative data against if it is to be of any value. These are usually:

- comparative figures for *other* individuals, groups, or organisations
- past comparative figures for the *same* individual, group, or organisation
- a target or objective.

On the face of it, making such comparisons should be quite straightforward. A target is either met or it is not met: Person or Department A's output is lower than B's; we did better this month than last. However, in recent years the work of the American statistician and 'quality guru',[1] W Edwards Deming, has shown that such easy comparisons can be very misleading. Consider this newspaper report:

> Shocking figures from Sheffield schools show that half our children are performing below average.

Of course they are. *By definition*, except in all but the most extreme situations,[2] roughly half the people measured on any scale will be below average and the other half above average. To take another example, say we have 10 people in a department being assessed by the number of errors they make per thousand items they produce. *By definition*, one person (10 per cent) is bound to be better than all the others, and therefore in the top 10 per cent, and one is going to be bottom, and therefore in the bottom 10 per cent. This is an inescapable fact. In any system of this nature, someone (or some group) is bound to be 'top' and another is bound to be 'bottom'. So merely ranking people and making decisions based on these ranks is completely misleading – even though it forms the basis of many current appraisal schemes.

In order to find out what differences in performance are telling us we have to see how significant they are. And to do this we have to understand a bit about the nature of differences in output, or variation, from a system.

Variation in a system

Take a very simple case: say, a typing pool where a group of eight secretaries provides assistance to a team of people. Each secretary's performance is the net result of a whole host of factors, including of course their skills and competencies, but also the nature of the workload, the person they are doing the work for, the equipment and procedures used, and so on. So the typist's output – measured, let's say, by errors per 5,000 words of typing – is the result of all those factors in what we call the secretary-typing system as a whole. Therefore, if we are comparing the output of each typist, we are really comparing the output of the whole secretary-typist system, as a whole, each typist being just one part of it.

Now inevitably, as already stated, individual performances differ. What we have to do is see whether there is any *significant* difference between the work of each typist. As an example, take the case in Table 5.

Table 5

TYPISTS' ERRORS

Typist	Number of mistakes per 5,000 words (over the previous month)
A	14
B	15
C	11
D	4
E	17
F	23
G	11
H	12
	Total 107

Now we have already seen that, inevitably, one employee will be in the top 12½ per cent (ie first out of eight or ⅛); and similarly one will be in the bottom 12½ per cent. But how significant is this information? At first sight, typist F is pretty poor – probably needs training, or something. But look at good old D – a star performer! But is this true? To find out, we have to bring in the dreaded s-word – statistics!

Many of us – the writers of this book included – have had a bad formative experience with statistics, or for other reasons are convinced that we cannot work with them.

However, they can be exceedingly useful, and need not be too difficult. So let us try. We urge you to read through the following process.

First, we can plot a chart of the performance data, as shown in Figure 10.

Figure 10

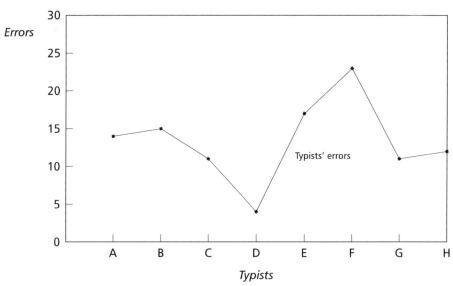

TYPISTS' ERRORS
(Data from Table 5)

Next we calculate the average, or mean, of the error scores, by dividing the total errors (107) by the number of typists (8). Thus

mean number of errors = 107 ÷ 8 = 13.38

We draw this line on the chart, as in Figure 11. Incidentally, note that four people (C, D, G, and H) are better than average, and four (A, B, E, and F) are worse. Yet again, 'half our typists are worse than the average' – *by definition, of course they are*!

Figure 11

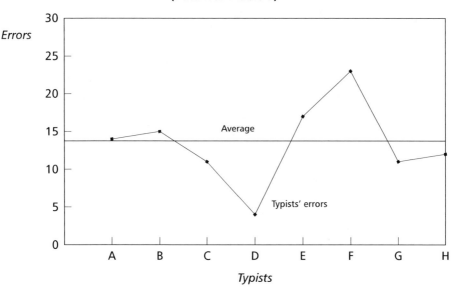

AVERAGE FOR TYPISTS' ERRORS
(Data from Table 5)

Now for the 'tricky' bit! Strictly speaking, we need to calculate what is known as the standard deviation. This can be a bit difficult (although computers and calculators will do it for us easily), but fortunately *for the type of data used here*[3] an approximation can be used. This is the square root of the mean. So in this case we have

$$\text{Square-root of mean} \quad = \quad \sqrt{13.38}$$
$$= \quad 3.66$$

Now we multiply this by 3:

$$3.66 \times 3 \quad = \quad 10.98$$

and calculate what are known as the upper control limit (given by $13.38 + 10.98 = 24.36$) and lower control limit (given by $13.38 - 10.98 = 2.40$). We now draw lines, as in Figure 12 (on page 66), at 24.36 and 2.40.

Now any points between these limits are said to be *in control*, ie, *they cannot be said to be significantly different from one another*. As far as we can tell from the data available, any difference or variation between them is due to 'random' occurrences or else natural variation within the system. So even typist F, at 23 errors, is still within the control limits. *There is no evidence to suggest that typist F's performance is significantly worse than the others'*. This may seem surprising, but it is true! So suggestions for training typist F (or punishing her, or taking other individually oriented remedial action) are not justified and will not work.

Figure 12

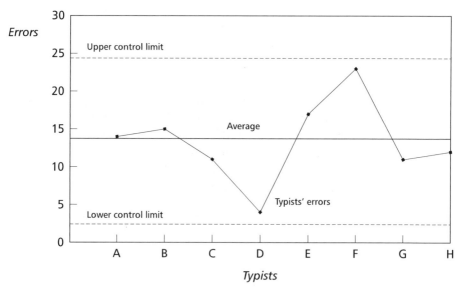

TYPISTS' ERRORS, SHOWING CONTROL LIMITS
(Data from Table 5)

In such a case, *where the system is in control, performance will be raised only if we look at the system as a whole and improve it*. This makes it a level I_2 or improving need, which *may* mean training *all* typists. However, if so, it will mean different training from that which they have already received, which is part of the current system.

Now suppose typist F's performance were 30 errors, not 23. The calculations are as follows:

Mean errors		$= (14 + 15 + 11 + 4 + 17 + 30 + 11 + 12) \div 8$
	$=$	14.25
Square root of mean	$=$	$\sqrt{14.25} = 3.78$
Upper control limit	$=$	mean $+ 3 \times \sqrt{\text{mean}}$
	$=$	$14.25 + 3 \times 3.78$
	$=$	25.59
Lower control limit	$=$	mean $- 3 \times \sqrt{\text{mean}}$
	$=$	$14.25 - 3 \times 3.78$
	$=$	2.91

Drawing these as in Figure 13 (on page 68) shows that typist F *is* now outside the upper control limit and therefore cannot be considered part of the same system as the others. There *is* evidence that something special – *a special cause* of variation – is happening. When a point falls outside the control limits, then the system is said to be not in control, and those points outside are considered 'special causes'. Their performance can be improved by focusing specifically on them and taking individual remedial action (which may include training). As we have seen, we can link this with what we saw in Chapter 1. If a point is outside the control limits, it is a special cause and individual action to bring it to the standard of the system as a whole is needed. This means a need at level I_1: implementing. If all points are within the control limits,[4] then there is no point in focusing on any individual. Instead, improvement can be made only by looking at the system as a whole. This means a need at level I_2: improving.

Figure 13

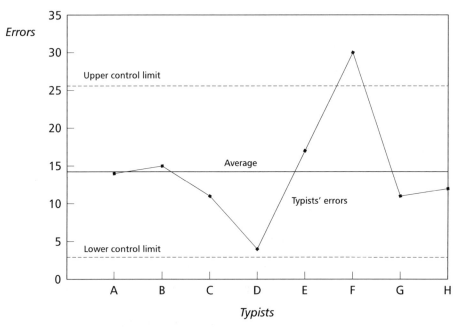

TYPISTS' ERRORS – REVISED DATA

Typist F lies outside the upper control limit, thus justifying individual remedial action. (Data modified from Table 5)

The example given above was very simple, where the control limits were simply given by:

$$\text{Upper control limit} = \text{mean} + 3 \times \sqrt{\text{mean}}$$

$$\text{Lower control limit} = \text{mean} - 3 \times \sqrt{\text{mean}}$$

For many cases where we are measuring numbers of errors this will suffice. A more general formula involves calculating the standard deviation of the data (which can easily be done using a statistical calculator) and multiplying this by three. If you cannot face that, then at least draw a chart and, before picking out individuals, make a visual check to see whether they appear 'in control'. This will be better than simply saying that the people at the bottom end must necessarily be significantly worse, and therefore in need of training, although it is still much better to do the calculation.

This whole area is one of great importance. All too often, individuals have been picked out as being poor performers when their scores represented just the natural, random variation that *will always occur* in any system. Treating them as special cases (or special causes, to use the statistical term) is a waste of time and effort, and often makes things worse. To handle this, then, we suggest the following:

(a) Draw a graph of the overall performance of all the people (or teams, units, or whatever) involved.

(b) Calculate the average or mean, and draw it in.

(c) Ideally, calculate the standard deviation, either by using the strict definition, or a calculator or computer with built-in statistical functions, or by using an approximation formula from a textbook on quality improvement (eg Wheeler and Chambers 1991).

(d) Draw the upper and lower control limits, given by the formula:

Upper control limit = mean + (3 × standard deviation)

Lower control limit = mean − (3 × standard deviation)

Remember that, usually, a lower control limit of less than zero is treated as zero.

(e) Proceed as already described – ie people outside the control limits are special cases/causes, and *may* be helped by individual remedial training. People inside the control limits will not be helped by individual remedial training. Instead, to improve their performance, the whole system must be looked at; if training is a solution then *everybody* will need improved training.

(f) If you really cannot use any method for calculating control limits, then try to estimate by eye. But this is difficult and may well lead to erroneous conclusions.

You may think that this is all rather a nuisance. Well, perhaps it is a bit of a challenge but, if you do not do it, you will probably do more harm than good by drawing quite erroneous conclusions from apparently 'obvious' figures that actually are not obvious at all. Deming himself put this rather starkly when somebody asked if it was really necessary to go to this trouble. 'No, you don't have to,' said Deming. 'Survival is not compulsory.'

Comparisons over a period of time

All too often people jump into a frenzy of activity (or of self-congratulation) because 'output's up' ie the figures are better this month than last (or than for the same month last year). Unfortunately, though, just as one swallow does not make a summer, so one month's change (deterioration or improvement) does not mean anything. Indeed, given random processes at work, it is actually more likely to be up or down than to remain constant. Happily, there are some simple graphical processes – not involving calculations as such – that can indicate whether a change is significant. These were invented by Lloyd Nelson, and are hence known as the Nelson Rules. They require seven constructive measurements ie over a period of seven days, seven weeks, seven months, or even seven quarters. However, that is a fact of life: you can tell whether a trend has set in only after a reasonable period of time – *seven* time periods, in fact.

Let us take the output from a particular group. We have data from 18 months, in which month 10 would appear to be pivotal (Figures 14 and 15). What does the data tell us? You can say that a significant trend has happened if you have

■ seven *consecutive* points each of which is higher than the one before (upward trend)

■ seven *consecutive* points each of which is *lower* than the one before (downward trend).

Figure 14 shows an upward trend starting at month 10, because after that the next seven points are all higher than the one before. Similarly, Figure 15 shows a downward trend, again starting at month 10, because each of the next seven points is lower than the one before.

Figure 14

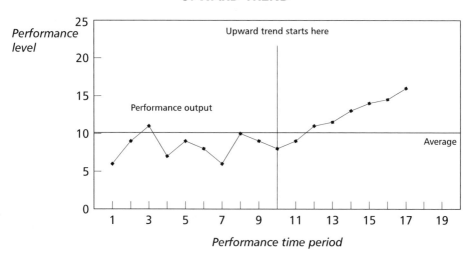

Figure 15

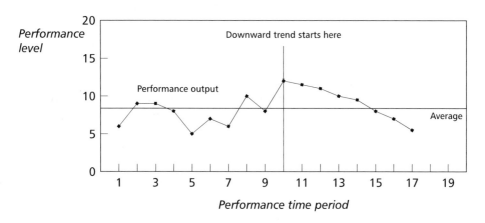

Similarly, you can say that a significant run has happened if:

■ seven consecutive points lie above the mean (upward run)

■ seven consecutive points lie below the mean (downward run)

So Figure 16 shows what is called an upward run, starting at month 9, because the following points are all above the mean. And Figure 17 shows a downward run, starting at month 10, because the next seven points are all below the mean.

Figure 16

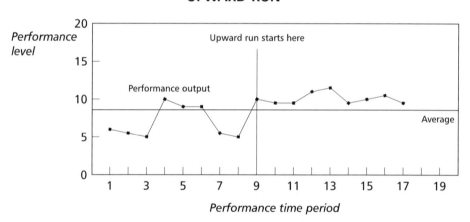

UPWARD RUN

Once a trend or a run is established, *then* we can say that 'fings ain't what they used to be', look for *reasons*, and determine whether training may help – either by devising a better training programme for everybody in previous work methods, or by devising new methods and then training everybody in these.

Figure 17

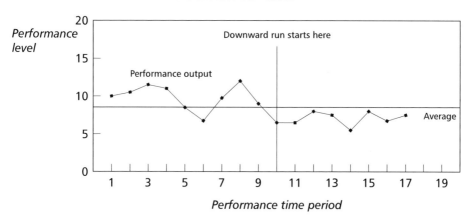

DOWNWARD RUN

Performance time period

Using the Nelson Rules to compare different individuals

We saw earlier in this chapter that if we have one-shot data of people's performance, then, to see whether or not there are any significant differences between them, we have to find out whether any individual's scores lie outside the control limits. However, if we have data on a number of individuals over a period of time, we can also use the Nelson Rules. Take the example in Table 6 (on page 74) of production data for six people over a period of eight weeks. The question arises whether any of the people are special cases – ie is remedial action required for any one or more individuals? Prime candidates are, of course, A and C, whose output looks quite a lot lower than that of their colleagues. However, rather than rely on a quick visual check, we can plot a graph of weekly output for each person, as in Figure 18 (on page 74), which includes the mean (ie average): which is $416 \div 48$, or 8.67. You will see that each person's scores are identified in clusters. Using the Nelson Rules that seven or more consecutive points below (or above) the mean, signify a special case, we see that:

■ person A is *not* a special case
■ person C *is* a special case.

Table 6

PRODUCTION DATA

Person	Week								Total
	1	*2*	*3*	*4*	*5*	*6*	*7*	*8*	
A	5	4	10	8	4	9	11	8	59
B	8	10	9	9	8	9	12	9	74
C	4	6	3	5	7	4	4	7	40
D	12	8	9	10	13	11	7	8	78
E	14	12	10	9	8	6	11	10	80
F	13	10	6	11	8	14	12	11	85
Total	56	50	47	52	48	53	57	53	416

Figure 18

USING THE NELSON RULES FOR COMPARISON
(Data from Table 6)

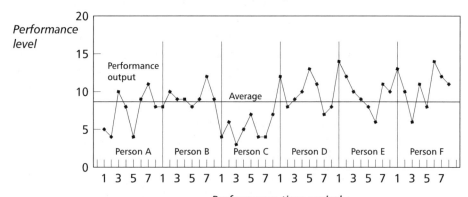

Therefore, some remedial action for person C is justified (which may or may not include training). Person C has a level I_1: implementing need. Person A, on the other hand, is part of the whole system: his or her relatively low output is just part of the 'random' natural variation that the system contains. Individual attention to A will be a wasted effort.

If we want A's performance to improve, then we need to look at the system as a whole and find ways in which everyone's performance may get better (a level I_2: improving need). This may involve new methods and equipment, or indeed training – not further training of the type previously carried out, but an entirely new, redesigned and improved training programme for everybody.

To many trainers these statistical procedures will seem unnecessary and complex. So, to clarify matters, let us first summarise them.

1 Data should be plotted on a graph to look for special cases, which exist if

  ▮ points lie outside the control limits (defined by mean $\pm$ three standard deviations)

  ▮ seven consecutive points increase, or decrease, or lie above or below the mean (the Nelson Rules).

2 If a special case exists, then remedial action for that individual is justified, which may include retraining.

3 If a special case does not exist, then the only way to bring about improvements is to work on the whole system, which may include designing a new, improved training programme for everyone.

If these simple rules are followed, then training will be in a much stronger position to play a real part in improving business performance. If they are not followed, then training may well be a waste of effort, and indeed is quite likely to make things worse. This may sound far-fetched, but it is a very important lesson that we trainers and HR people can learn – indeed must learn – from our colleagues in quality and continuous improvement.

Comparison against a target

Individuals, departments, and organisations are often given performance targets to achieve; the extent to which they do so is then used for appraisal, reward or punishment, and identification of needs. Yet all too often these targets are used by people who do not understand the points we made earlier in this chapter about natural variation in a system.

For example, let us return to the typist case. Suppose the company set a target, *for the department as a whole*, of no more than 15 errors per 2,000 words. In Figure 19, this target has been drawn in. It is in fact a lower standard (ie more errors) than the *average* performance of all the typists. Therefore the current target, for the department as a whole, is achievable and is being achieved. Of course, certain individuals (E and F) are doing worse than the target. But as we have already seen, these two are still within the control limits, and their 'worse' performance is part of the inevitable variation that the system as a whole is *bound* to produce. This means, as before, that taking individual action to try to bring these two within the target level will be a wasted effort.

Figure 19

TYPISTS' ERRORS WITH DEPARTMENTAL TARGET
(Data from Table 5)

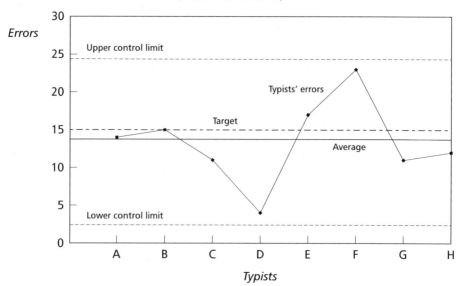

If we really do want *everybody* in the unit to achieve that level of target, then we have to redesign the methods and systems – including training – so that the target is now greater than the upper control limit. If this happens, then we can say that in principle *everybody* will achieve the target, and that if specific individuals do not, then remedial action will be justified.

In the case we are looking at, suppose a decision has been made that indeed *nobody* must make more than 15 errors per 5,000 words. As already shown, this means that new processes and methods are going to be required. By using some of the techniques described later (especially brainstorming, nominal group technique, Pareto analysis and fishbone, see Chapter 5), it was decided that the following main changes would be particularly helpful:

1 changing the working structure, so that each typist worked for a limited number of managers and therefore became more familiar with their handwriting
2 activating the spell-checker in the word processing program – previously it had not been used
3 giving all typists additional training in how to use the spell-checker.

The results can be seen in Table 7 on page 78 (repeating the earlier figures for the previous month [Table 5] in column A). (Incidentally, note that three are still worse than average, three better than average, and two average!)

These figures are plotted in Figure 20. The new upper and lower limits are shown, namely:

$$5 + 3 \times \sqrt{5} \quad = 11.71$$

$$5 - 3 \times \sqrt{5} \quad = -1.71 = \text{zero (it is not possible to have fewer than zero errors)}$$

So the new target – no one to make more than 15 errors – is worse than the control limits. *Everybody* will achieve it

Table 7

TYPISTS' ERRORS (ii)

Typist	A Mistakes per 5,000 words in month prior to change	B Mistakes per 5,000 words in month after change
A	14	4
B	15	6
C	11	3
D	4	5
E	17	4
F	23	5
G	11	7
H	12	6
Total 107		40
Average 13.38		5.00

Figure 20

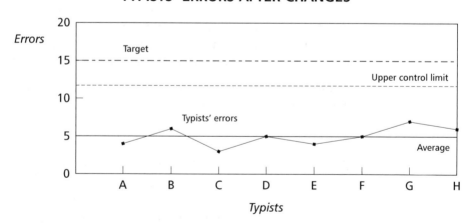

TYPISTS' ERRORS AFTER CHANGES

and department output as a whole will average 5.00 errors. And yet again (looking at Figure 20) three typists make fewer errors than average, three more than average, and one makes the average. If you set an overall target that is the same as the average individual performance, then about half the people will not meet that target. This is inevitable!

A note on presenting data

If you have gone through this chapter systematically, you will have been introduced to a variety of different ways of presenting collected data that is extremely useful in ITN. We strongly recommend that, whenever possible, the information you gather is presented in ways that are attractive, easy to follow, and obvious to interpret – for your own benefit as well as that of anyone else involved. Looking back over Chapter 4 (and Chapters 1 to 3), make a list (another way of presenting data) of the various ways in which data has been presented here and then see which ones might be most useful for you to use. (More presentation methods appear in subsequent chapters.)

In brief

This chapter is an important one for learning about ITN, because it introduces what is perhaps a new approach – learning to apply techniques that have proved their worth in other fields, particularly quality improvement, but that have as yet not been used to full advantage by training specialists. If we can use these techniques (which involve new ways of thinking about training and ITN), we shall have better ways of analysing, presenting and interpreting data collected for ITN purposes.

A starting-point for data-based ITN is the appropriate use of thinking about people and tasks, based on making suitable comparisons. This seems an obvious thing to do, but, as we have seen, the obvious is not always the most commonly applied. Unless we include comparisons we shall be unable accurately to identify real differences between current performance and what is required, or what we need to do to enhance performance. Furthermore, by using suitable comparisons we might avoid some of the all too common distortions and traps involved in using data. So now we know how to:

- ascertain where comparative data is needed as part of an ITN process
- use data based on comparisons for analysis, presentation, and interpretation
- assess performance by being able to calculate a mean, work out standard deviations, and, most significantly, plot upper and lower control limits from this.
- judge whether a system is in control or not
- distinguish between special and common causes of variation in a system (and their relationship to I_1: implementing and I_2: improving levels of performance
- ensure that we do not attribute poor performance to random variation (ie variation that will always occur in any system and about which we can do little) and therefore draw erroneous conclusions from the data.

As we have seen, comparisons can be used to illustrate clearly:

- how things change over a period of time, using simple graphic means such as the Nelson Rules which enable us to see distinct trends
- the differences in individual performance
- the achievement of performance targets for individuals, departments, and aspects of the organisation as a whole.

Reference

WHEELER DJ AND CHAMBERS DS *Understanding Statistical Process Control*. Knoxville; 2nd edn, SPC Inc, 1991.

The British Deming Association (The Old George Brewery, Rollestone Street, Salisbury SP1 1DX) supplies this and a number of other books on statistical process control.

End-notes

1 In fact Deming himself rarely referred to quality as such, but to continuous improvement. However, he is seen by others as a leader of the 'quality movement'.

2 Where the distribution is markedly skewed.

3 This approximation is valid where there are many opportunities for errors to occur, and where the actual occurrence of an error is rare; also the occurrence of an error by one person must not cause another person to make an error at the same time.

4 Sometimes the lower control limit is less than zero. This is treated as zero – after all, it is impossible to make a minus number of errors!

Analysing Training Needs

Summary of the overall process

In this chapter we shall look at an overall process for the deeper analysis of areas where there is some preliminary evidence (such as objective data, feedback from others, internal surveys, and so on, as described in Chapter 2) to suggest that a training need may exist. This process can in principle be used any level of need and with any focus (ie organisational, group, or individual). At the same time we shall describe some basic techniques to help with the analysis.

This overall process is as follows:

1   Define and chart that part of the organisation in which you work

> *Useful technique*: flow chart (described in this chapter)

2   Collect more data to shed light on what is going on

> *Useful techniques*: the various data-collecting methods described throughout this book. Also Pareto analysis – described in this chapter.

3   Where appropriate, analyse data using control charts.

> *Useful technique*: control chart, described in Chapter 4.

4   Find out the causes of the problems, which may include needs for training.

Useful techniques: observation, involvement, fish-bone, and brainstorming – described in this chapter.

5   Prioritise the causes.

Useful technique: nominal group technique, described in this chapter.

6   Propose and prioritise possible solutions.

Useful technique: brainstorming and nominal group technique can also be used here.

Step 1: define and chart that part of the organisation in which you work

Whatever level of need, focus, or type of data you will have to define the boundaries of that part of the system you are investigating.

Defining the boundaries

These boundaries may typically be:

■ a particular department, section, or unit
■ a specific group or staff category
■ a given process.

Often these will overlap. For example, in a restaurant kitchen (*unit*) the food preparation (*process*) is carried out by kitchen staff (*staff category*). At other times, processes will overlap several sections, or involve more than one staff category. So if we took the restaurant as a whole, we would have:

■ units   – kitchen, dining-room, car park
■ staff   – chefs, waiters, cloakroom attendants, car park attendants
■ processes – preparing food, washing up, laying tables, taking orders, serving food, clearing up, running the cloakroom, helping in the car park.

You will have to decide on the scope of your survey and then identify the broad categories – the three Ps of Place, People, Process – that you are going to study.

Charting the process

Once you have done this, we suggest you draw up a simple flow chart of the process. Taking the restaurant example, this might look something like Figure 21.

Figure 21

SIMPLE FLOW CHART (i)

Customer arrives
↓
Customer helped to park car
↓
Customer gives coat
to cloakroom attendant
↓
Customer greeted
in restaurant
↓
Customer orders meal
↓
Meal cooked
↓
Meal served
↓
Bill presented and paid
↓
Customer collects coat
↓
Customer enters car
and drives away

Figure 22

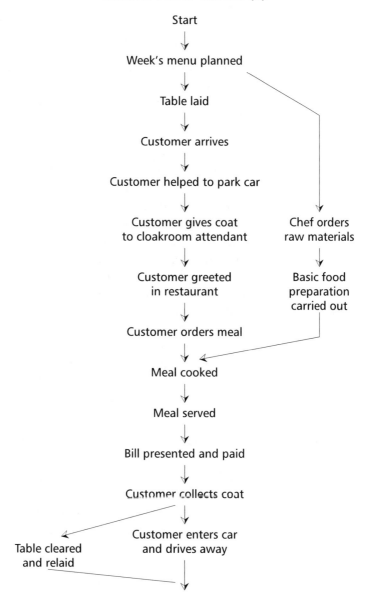

SIMPLE FLOW CHART (ii)

Start

Week's menu planned

Table laid

Customer arrives

Customer helped to park car

Customer gives coat   Chef orders
to cloakroom attendant   raw materials

Customer greeted   Basic food
in restaurant   preparation
                             carried out

Customer orders meal

Meal cooked

Meal served

Bill presented and paid

Customer collects coat

Table cleared   Customer enters car
and relaid   and drives away

This is the flow of the process from the *customer's* point of view. However, it omits various important steps from the *organisation's* point of view. For example, how does the chef know what raw materials to obtain? Figure 22 (on page 85) illustrates this process.

This version contains other information, for example about planning the menu and ordering food in advance. However, it may be more useful to present it in a slightly different way – one that clearly differentiates between the staff categories involved, as in Figure 23. This version, which is sometimes known as an integrated flow chart, allows for more detail, shows things that go on at the same time as one another, and clearly indicates the part that each staff category plays in the whole process. Furthermore, lines going across the chart show interfaces between one staff category (or department) and another. For example, it is clear that the restaurant manager and the chef have to get together (a horizontal line) to plan the week's menu – ⓐ on Figure 23. Sloping cross-lines show where there is a flow from one unit to another. So we have the flow of information about the customer's order from restaurant to kitchen ⓑ and about the order being ready from kitchen to restaurant ⓒ. Similarly, the waiter has to 'flow' to the kitchen to pick up the meal ⓓ and then take it back into the restaurant ⓔ.

Redefining the boundaries of the system you are working on

Having drawn a picture of the overall process, you will need to decide which part you want to concentrate on. This will largely depend on what information you already have and why you think there is a problem. For example, if your information is that kitchen costs are rising, you might reasonably expect to focus on the *kitchen staff* line of the chart. However, we suggest that at the very least you would look, in such a case, not only at the direct kitchen process, but also at where it interfaces with other subsystems – in this case the restaurant. This is because problems in one part of the overall system are very often

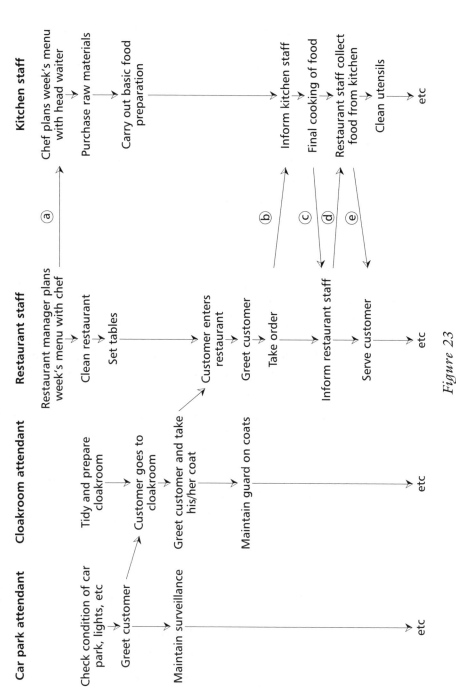

Figure 23

INTEGRATED FLOW CHART

being caused elsewhere. Here, for example, it may be that the head waiter is overruling the chef and insisting on a menu that contains very exotic – and expensive – out-of-season delicacies, such as fresh asparagus in January for a UK restaurant.

Drawing a more detailed flow chart

At this point you might find it helpful to draw a more detailed flow chart. This may well use a symbol for 'decision point', – usually a diamond shape. An example is shown in Figure 24 opposite.

Step 2: collect more data

Whether you use a relatively broad-brush flow chart, or a more detailed one, you will now need to investigate further. You can use the flow chart as a guide for collecting more data. For example, if the triggering symptom for your investigation was a high, or rising, level of customer complaint, you would obviously need to find out what the complaints are about.

In general, you can collect both quantitative and qualitative data about most of the main parts of the process you have drawn. In our example this could include:

Quantitative data
- How long does it take for the kitchen to receive the customer's order?
- How does this differ according to the waiter involved?
- How long does it take to prepare the meal?
- How does this differ according to the items ordered?
- How does this differ according to the cooks involved?
- How much delay is there between the meal's being ready and its being served to the customer?
- How does this differ according to the staff involved?

Figure 24

DETAILED FLOW CHART FOR PURCHASING RAW MATERIALS

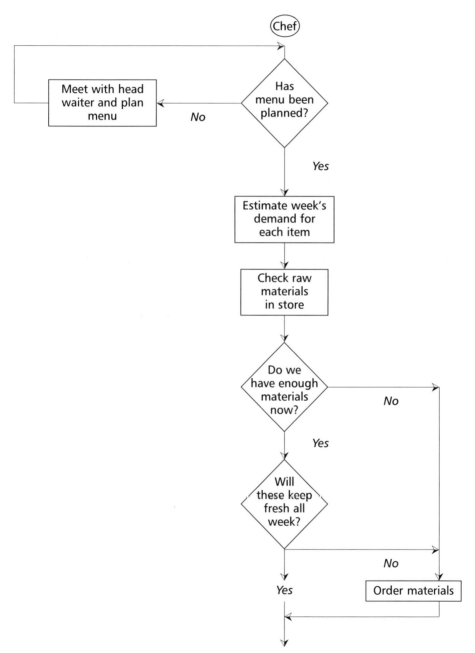

Figure 25

TONGUE-IN-CHEEK FLOW CHART

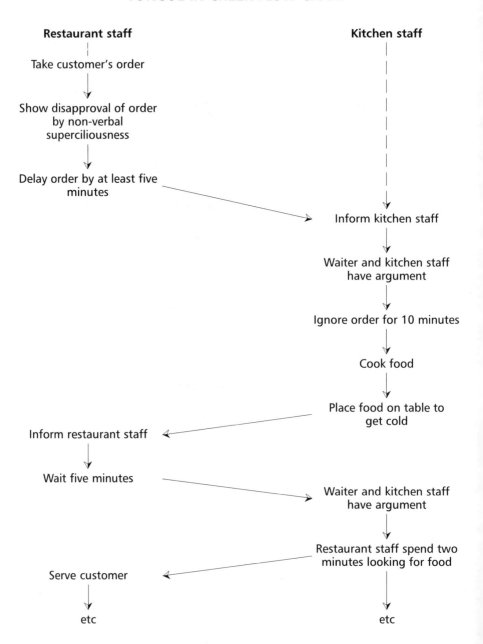

■ How far do the staff have to walk or does the food have to travel?

■ How much raw material is wasted or thrown away?

Qualitative data   ■ How would you describe the relationship between the kitchen staff and the restaurant staff?

■ What is the match between customer expectations and menu offered (eg are they expecting fast food and being offered individually prepared *haute cuisine*)?

At this point you may find it rather instructive – and in a way quite fun – to draw what we shall call a *tongue-in-cheek flow chart* (Figure 25). This draws the process as in fact it is being carried out, rather than how it should be. All errors, delays, and so on are written in as though they are part of the actual process.

A tongue-in-cheek flow chart does show what is happening in reality. It makes a good point when you are presenting the results of your analysis.

Pareto analysis

Pareto analysis is a useful way of finding out which aspect of improvement is most urgent. Consider the restaurant again. There have been rising complaints from customers. What are these complaints about? On investigation, you find that over the past three months the complaints have been as laid out in Table 8 on page 92.

Obviously, three main complaints stand out: delays (28.1 per cent), smoking (18.8 per cent) and undercooked vegetables (12.5 per cent). Between them these three give rise to 59.4 per cent of all complaints. So just over 59 per cent of complaints are associated with just three of the 11 causes (ie 27 per cent of causes).

This phenomenon, whereby a small percentage of causes gives rise to a large proportion of the actual problems, is known as the Pareto effect, after an Italian economist who

Table 8

RESTAURANT COMPLAINTS

		Number of complaints	% of total complaints
1	Meat undercooked	15	9.4
2	Food too cold	10	6.3
3	Food too rich	15	9.4
4	Delays between ordering and receiving food	45	28.1
5	Restaurant too hot	5	3.1
6	Restaurant too cold	3	1.9
7	Vegetables undercooked	20	12.5
8	Vegetables overcooked	2	1.2
9	Smoking allowed in restaurant	30	18.8
10	Prices too high	10	6.2
11	Others	5	3.1
		160	100.0

noticed that 80 per cent of his country's wealth lay in the hands of 20 per cent of the population. Although it is easy to spot the effect just by looking at the figures, it is often useful to plot them as a Pareto chart (Figure 26), where you will see the causes or problems presented in descending order. As well as helping with analysis, charts like this can be very useful when sharing your findings either by writing a report or making a presentation.

Step 3: if appropriate, analyse data using control charts

In Chapter 4 we looked at the implications of using what we called control charts to analyse quantitative data. It may be useful to use a control chart at this stage of your analysis. In the case of the restaurant, for example, we might come up with something like Table 9.

Figure 26

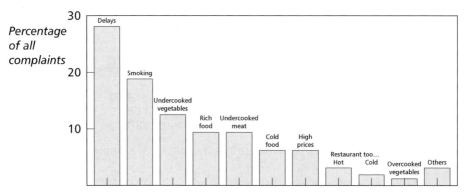

PARETO CHART

Nature of complaint

Table 9

DISH PREPARATION TIME (i)

Cook	Average time to prepare a certain dish over the past month (minutes)
A	10
B	4
C	15
D	8
E	6
F	3
G	4
H	7
Average =	57 ÷ 8 = 7.13 minutes

On the face of it, cook C is rather poor compared with the others. Should we take remedial action such as retraining, or even taking C off that particular job? Using the control chart technique described in Chapter 4, we get the following:

Average time that
all cooks take to
prepare dish   = 7.13 minutes

Standard deviation = 3.94 minutes
(using a calculator)

Upper control limit = average + 3 × standard deviation

= 7.13 + 3 × 3.94

= 18.95 minutes

Lower control limit = average − 3 × standard deviation

= 7.13 − 3 × 3.94

= − 4.69 minutes

(which counts as zero, because you
cannot have a negative time to
prepare a dish!)

It will be seen that chef C still lies within the control limits
(Figure 27) and therefore is not a special case. From the
data available, individual remedial action is not justified;
indeed it might make things worse.

Figure 27

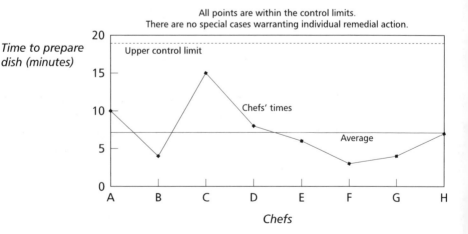

RESTAURANT EXAMPLE (i)

All points are within the control limits.
There are no special cases warranting individual remedial action.

*Time to prepare
dish (minutes)*

Upper control limit

Chefs' times

Average

Chefs

Here is another example. Suppose now the times are those in Table 10.

Table 10

DISH PREPARATION TIME (ii)

Cook	Average time to prepare a certain dish
A	12
B	12
C	11
D	13
E	35
F	11
G	12
H	11
I	13
J	12
K	13
L	14
M	12

Average $= \overline{181} \div 13 = 13.92$ minutes

Standard deviation $= 6.40$ minutes

Upper control limit $=$ average $+ 3 \times$ standard deviation

$$= 13.92 + 3 \times 6.40$$

$$= 33.12 \text{ minutes}$$

Lower control limit $=$ average $- 3 \times$ standard deviation

$$= 13.92 - 3 \times 6.40$$

$$= -5.28 \text{ minutes}$$

(which again counts as zero)

In this case chef E *is* outside the control limits (Figure 28) and therefore his or her performance *can* be said to be significantly different from that of the others. Individual remedial action is justified – which might call for retraining, although there may be other factors to investigate as well.

Figure 28

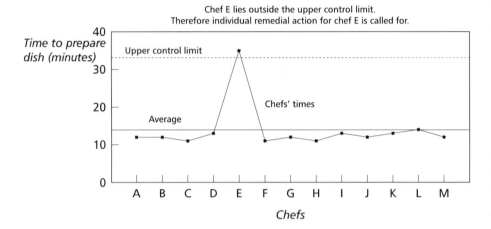

RESTAURANT EXAMPLE (ii)

Chef E lies outside the upper control limit.
Therefore individual remedial action for chef E is called for.

Time to prepare dish (minutes)

Upper control limit

Chefs' times

Average

Chefs

Step 4: find out the causes of the problems

From what we have just seen there may be a special case (or special cause), such as a particular person's needing retraining. Such special cases can be dealt with individually on their merits. However, when we have *common* causes of unsatisfactory performance we have to look at the system as a whole in order to see what needs doing. A most valuable technique for this is known as the cause-and-effect diagram or, because of its shape, the fishbone. (It is also known as the Ishikawa diagram, after its inventor.)

The fishbone diagram

Although there are a number of versions of the fishbone, a typical one that will serve our purposes is shown in Figure 29. As you can see, the diagram consists of a number of lines or 'bones' that come together to cause the effect – in

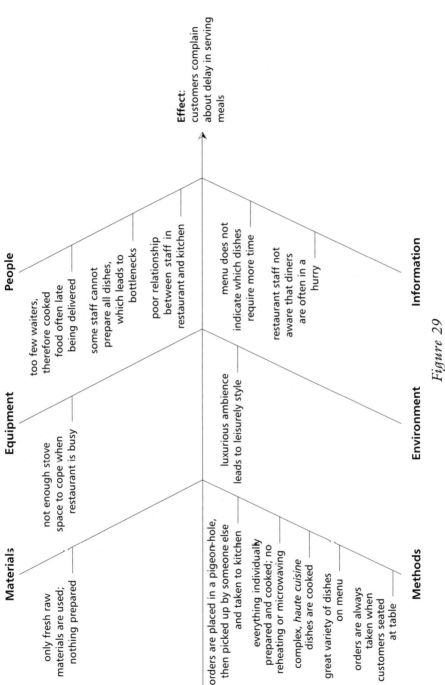

Figure 29
FISHBONE DIAGRAM

Materials
only fresh raw
materials are used;
nothing prepared

Equipment
not enough stove
space to cope when
restaurant is busy

People
too few waiters,
therefore cooked
food often late
being delivered

some staff cannot
prepare all dishes,
which leads to
bottlenecks

poor relationship
between staff in
restaurant and kitchen

Effect:
customers complain
about delay in serving
meals

orders are placed in a pigeon-hole,
then picked up by someone else
and taken to kitchen

everything individually
prepared and cooked; no
reheating or microwaving

complex, *haute cuisine*
dishes are cooked

great variety of dishes
on menu

orders are always
taken when
customers seated
at table

luxurious ambience
leads to leisurely style

menu does not
indicate which dishes
require more time

restaurant staff not
aware that diners
are often in a
hurry

Methods

Environment

Information

this case, customers complaining of a delay in being served their meal. Note the way this is worded: it does *not* say 'delays in serving meals' but quite deliberately says that 'customers complain of a delay'. This is because that is how the problem shows itself. This version of the diagram has six main 'bones' or clusters of cause. These are materials, equipment, people, methods, environment, and information. Others can be used, but this is pretty much standard. You will see that some of the bones or clusters are more relevant to this particular example than others. This is often the case.

How do you actually find out what to put on the fishbone diagram – what the causes are? There are a number of ways.

Observation and involvement

The first way to find out what to put on the fishbone diagram is by observing what is going on and by talking to those involved – in this case, the kitchen and restaurant staff. These people – who work in the system – are the ones who really know what is going on, what is working and what is not. But rather than talking *to* them, talk *with* them; and perhaps get them involved in the process, so that they themselves are completing the fishbone, either with your help or indeed working on their own, as a team.

You may next find it useful to talk with other people – managers, experts, and the like. But, frankly, almost all the information you need will be found among those actually working within the system as internal suppliers and customers to one another. This is one of the big lessons from what we might call the continuous improvement movement.

Brainstorming

Brainstorming is another useful way of collecting opinions about what might be causing a problem. It can also be used to generate possible solutions. There are various ways of brainstorming, most of which are done in a group. We will describe three here. The first is as follows:

1   State clearly the issue under exploration, perhaps you can put it as a question beginning with 'what', 'why', or 'how'. For example, in our restaurant case we might simply state it thus:

> Why are we getting complaints from customers about the delay in serving their meals?

2   Check that all group members understand the question. Write it on a flip chart.

3   Give them two or three minutes to think about the question.

4   Ask for suggested answers. Write these on the flip chart. Use exactly the wording that people shout out – don't try to edit, shorten, or amplify what they say.

5   While suggestions are being shouted out, make sure there is no comment, criticism, praise, or any evaluative or judgemental response. This helps to create an atmosphere in which people feel able to make their contributions, no matter how strange, unusual, idiosyncratic, counter-culture or tabu-busting they appear to be. This means that non-verbal reactions, such as laughter, groans, cries of amazement, strong gestures, and so on are not allowed either!

6   About 10 minutes is usually sufficient to get a long enough list.

7   Go through all the items on the chart, asking whether anybody does not understand them. If so, the person who suggested that item explains what was meant.

8   Go through the list to see whether there is any duplication. If two items appear to be the same, then check with the people who suggested them. If they *both* agree that they are indeed the same, then these items can be combined.

Another method of brainstorming is to allow a bit more time at the start and ask each group member to write their solutions on a piece of paper. Then go round the group in turn, asking each person to call out *one* idea from his/her list and to cross off any idea that someone else has already called out. Keep going round until everyone has called out all their ideas.

A third method also involves writing down ideas on a piece of paper, say, for three minutes. Members then pass their papers to the person on their right, and, after reading the ideas on the paper they have just received, add any more that are triggered off. After another three minutes or so, papers are passed on again. The process continues until the papers return to their originators. Then the ideas are read out and put on the flip chart. This method is suitable for relatively small groups, say, three to eight people.

When brainstorming you can 'freewheel' and then cluster the ideas onto a fishbone, using either the standard 'bones' or new ones to suit your particular situation. Alternatively, you can draw the outline fishbone and then use each part of it as a trigger for your brainstorming.

Step 5: prioritise the causes

Once you have identified a number of causes of the particular problem, you will then have to decide how to handle them. Many of them will be outside your sphere of authority or influence. For example, as a trainer you will probably have little say over the nature and variety of the dishes on the menu. This is where the value of a good relationship between you and the others involved – chef, cooks, restaurant manager, waiters and so on – shows itself. Ideally, all the reasons will be explored in more detail and various actions taken.

As someone interested in training, your own tendency would be to act on two of the 'people' reasons, namely:

▮ kitchen staff are somewhat slow in preparing food

▮ some staff cannot prepare all dishes, which leads to bottlenecks.

It may well be that you can usefully take action on these independently of anything that is also done to tackle some of the other causes. However, if you *can* work collaboratively to get a picture of which of these causes are most relevant or urgent, then so much the better.

Nominal group technique

This method is highly suitable for a group of between five and 25 members. The process is as follows:

1   On a flip chart, prepare a grid, with all the items prioritised down one side and names of group members across the top.

2   Ask each group member, working individually, to choose what he or she thinks are the main, or most important, causes from the list. The number of main or most important causes they can choose will depend on the total number being considered. We would suggest something like this:

Total number of items	Number of main causes to choose
5	5
6 – 10	5 or 10
11 – 15	6
16 – 21	7 – 10
22 – 40	10 – 12

3   Each member then gives a score to his/her chosen top or main items. If he/she has chosen five in all, then the absolute top one gets five points. The second gets four, the third three, the fourth two, and the fifth one. Similarly, if he/she chooses 10 items in all, the first priority would get 10 points, the second nine, and so on. In this case the tenth would get one point.

4   Ask members to shout out their scores, and enter them on the chart. (In the restaurant example it might look like Table 11.)

Reason for delay	Person														Total	% of total	Rank
	Kitchen staff						Restaurant staff										
	A	B	C	D	E	F	G	H	I	J	K	L	M	N			
1 Using fresh raw materials														1	1	0.34	13
2 Not enough stove space when busy		5			1	3									9	3.06	9
3 Too few waiters							2	3	5			4		1	15	5.10	8
4 Some kitchen staff cannot prepare all dishes	5	6	3	6	5	6									31	10.54	5
5 Poor relationship between staff in restaurant and in kitchen	6		6			5		6	4		3	5		6	41	13.95	3
6 Menu does not indicate which dishes require more time	3	2	2	4	4	1	6	5	3	6	5	5	6	5	57	19.39	1
7 Restaurant staff not aware that diners are in a hurry										3	1		1		5	1.70	10
8 Luxurious ambience leads to leisurely style														2	2	0.68	11=
9 Pigeon-hole system for taking orders to kitchen	2		4	2	3	2	4	4	6	5	6	3	2	4	47	15.99	2
10 Everything individually prepared – no reheating										2					2	0.68	11=
11 Complex haute cuisine	4	3	5	5	6	4	1	1	2		2	2	3		38	12.93	4
12 Great variety of dishes on menu	1	4		3	2				1			1	4		16	5.44	7
13 Orders taken only when customers seated at table	1	1	1	1			3	2		4	4	6	5	3	30	10.20	6
															294	100.00	

Table 11

NOMINAL GROUP TECHNIQUE

As a check, the total number of points should equal the number of people (14) multiplied by the number of points each has available to allocate (in this case $6 + 5 + 4 + 3 + 2 + 1 = 21$). Thus the total should be:

$$14 \times 21 = 294$$

This is in fact the total in Table 11!

The scores are quite revealing. First, looked at overall, there are some clear 'winners' – or rather losers. These are:

Rank 1 Menu does not indicate which dishes require more time.

2 Pigeon-hole system for taking orders to kitchen.

3 Poor relationships between staff in restaurant and in kitchen.

4 Complex *haute cuisine*.

5 Some kitchen staff cannot prepare all dishes.

6 Orders taken only when customers are seated at table.

It should be noted, though, that if you were using just the scores of the kitchen staff, then their not all being able to prepare all dishes would actually be the number one priority reason. Similarly, for restaurant staff, on their own rating 'Orders taken only when customers seated at table' ranks fourth.

This illustrates a very important – and useful – feature of the nominal group technique. As well as showing the overall results or priorities, it also allows us to recognise differences between subgroups. Rather than ignoring these differences, we should acknowledge, respect, and value such alternative viewpoints. In this example, it is clear that the different subgroups have different information. In an important sense they are both 'right'.

Data from the nominal group technique often shows the Pareto effect that we have already described. This can be seen in Figures 30 to 32 on pages 104 to 105.

Figure 30

PARETO CHART
CAUSES OF DELAYS IN SERVING MEALS: DATA FROM KITCHEN STAFF

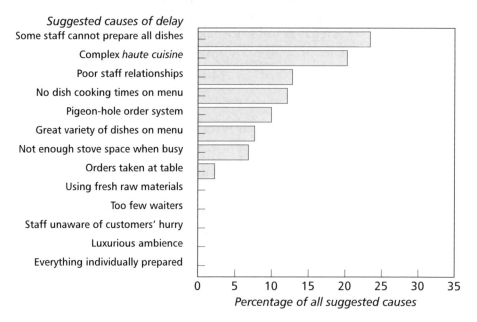

Figure 31

PARETO CHART
CAUSES OF DELAYS IN SERVING MEALS: DATA FROM RESTAURANT STAFF

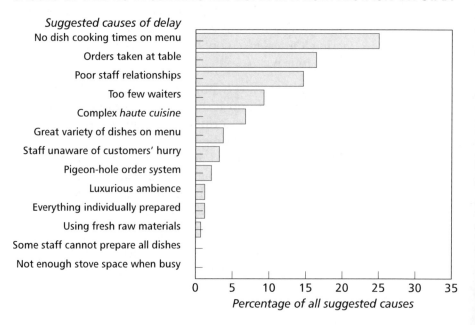

Figure 32

CAUSES OF DELAYS IN SERVING MEALS: DATA FROM ALL STAFF

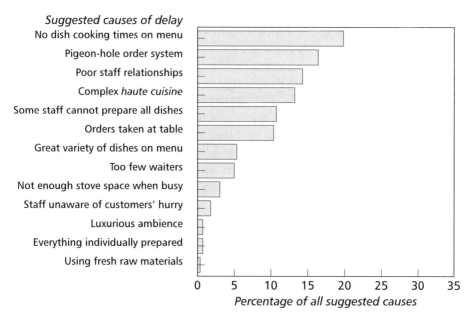

Step 6: propose and prioritise possible solutions

At this point you have identified a number of causes of a particular problem. In this case, the suggested main causes of customers complaining about delays in serving a meal have been seen to be:

Rank 1 Menu does not indicate which dishes require more time.

2 Pigeon-hole system for taking orders to kitchen.

3 Poor relationships between staff in restaurant and in kitchen.

4 Complex *haute cuisine*.

5 Some kitchen staff cannot prepare all dishes.

6 Orders taken only when customers are seated at table.

As someone responsible primarily for training, you may well feel that some of these – items 1, 2, 4, and 6 in particular – are not your concern. However, given that you do have overall concern, and indeed responsibility, for the success of the organisation, we suggest that you should feed this information back to those concerned and talk with them about it so that appropriate decisions on policy and operations can be made. Indeed, one of the things that has changed over the past few years is the way that 'trainers' see their role. Instead of restricting themselves to 'training' solutions – and therefore not seeing or responding to other causes – they now increasingly recognise their role as an internal consultant or facilitator, helping with problem-solving, change, and organisational learning, no matter what type of solution or intervention is called for.

Having decided what to do about these 'non-training' causes, this leaves two others of more direct relevance to training and HR interventions:

Rank 3 Poor relationships between staff in the restaurant and in the kitchen

        5 Some kitchen staff cannot prepare all dishes.

How you handle these is beyond our scope here. Clearly the second item lends itself to the possibility of direct training. Improving relationships between staff, on the other hand, may require a different type of intervention, such as setting up direct dialogue between the people involved. But that is for another book!

In brief

In this chapter we have concentrated on techniques and processes to analyse information gathered at previous stages of an ITN process. We have introduced techniques that enable us to move from initial diagnosis to more in-depth analysis, making decisions about which needs are really significant (and which are not), and thus focusing on solutions that will deliver real benefits.

These techniques help us therefore to investigate real

causes, generate possible solutions, and decide our priorities for training and learning. We can then be confident that training will work and that the pay-offs will be there for all to see. Remember, we began our introduction to ITN by saying that this was the kind of training we were really interested in. An investment in a thorough approach to ITN will give us the returns we are looking for. So we have examined techniques such as:

- *flow-charting* to focus on that part of the organisation we are really interested in, enabling us to describe and chart what is happening (and what should be happening) with greater clarity and precision

- *data presentation methods* (especially *Pareto*) to assist us in deciding which are the main causes of the problem

- *control charts* to identify where performance is significantly different, and where action is needed to remedy the situation

- *cause-and-effect diagrams* for examining the causes of unsatisfactory performance, difficulties, and shortfalls. Additional techniques such as *brainstorming* and *observation* can be used to generate a wider range of ideas about possible causes, involving others actively in the process.

- *prioritising* – an essential tool in the kitbag of any ITN practitioner. We can never use all solutions at once. We have to make choices, and this is where techniques such as the *nominal group technique* are most valuable, again involving others in the process.

Finally we come to the point where we need ideas about possible solutions. When we become solution-centred, the role of the trainer becomes more of an internal consultant or facilitator, dealing with the many influences on the organisation and finding a way through.

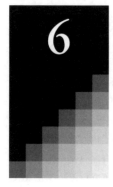

6 Focusing on Organisational Needs at Implementing and Improving Levels

At the end of Chapter 1 we drew up a table to bring the three focuses – organisational, group and individual – together with the three levels of learning and benefit – implementing, improving and innovating. That table is reproduced here, as Table 12. The shaded boxes show the topics we shall be looking at in this chapter. We shall look at organisational innovating needs in Chapter 7 – although, of course, data collected primarily for understanding how we are doing at implementing and improving levels may also highlight some needs at the innovating level.

Obviously, once an area of organisational need has been identified it will need further analysis before we can home in on the causes and hence possible solutions. From Chapter 1 you will recall that we are dealing here with situations where:

▌ either we are not meeting our current performance objectives (implementing)

▌ or we are achieving our *current* performance objectives but want to raise these to new levels (improving).

Using objective data

In Chapter 2 we saw that this involves quantitative data about a number of possible measures, including productivity, quality or delivery of a product or service, financial and commercial factors, personnel measures, and environmental data. Also you will recall from Chapter 4

Table 12

FOCUS OF CHAPTER 6

Area of need / Level of business benefit	Organisational	Group	Individual
I₁: Implementing – doing things well	Meeting current organisational objectives	Working together to meet existing targets and standards	Being competent at the level of existing requirements
I₂: Improving – doing things better	Setting higher objectives and reaching them	Continuous improvement teams	Having and using systematic, continuous improvement skills and processes
I₃: Innovating – doing new and better things	Changing objectives and strategies	Working across boundaries to create new relationships and new products and services	Being able to work differently and more creatively with a shared sense of purpose

that, to know anything meaningful about our performance, we have to compare this data with some reference point, namely with:

▌ comparative figures for other organisations

▌ past comparative figures for our own organisation

▌ a target or objective.

The last two points speak for themselves. But do remember that such comparisons are not always as straightforward as you might imagine. (We looked at this in some detail in Chapter 4.)

When it comes to making comparisons with other organisations an approach known as benchmarking can be useful.

Benchmarking

Benchmarking can be used to compare your performance with that of other organisations, including:

- ▊ *internal* – that is, with other parts of your own organisation, other establishments, branches, plants, and divisions. If this approach is appropriate it is the easiest, because access should be straightforward.

- ▊ *external, with a competitor.* This can be very useful if you can identify a competitor who you know – or just suspect – has the edge on you in one or more specific areas of performance. However, in practice it may be very difficult to get the data you want, although there are consultancies that specialise in trying to obtain information about competitors. You can also try trade journals, conferences, exhibitions, and so on. Another way to obtain information about a competitor is from customers – actually asking them how you shape up compared with your rivals.

  Finally, in a number of sectors you may be able to get some information by becoming a customer yourself – visiting a rival supermarket, hotel, restaurant, clothing store, or whatever.

- ▊ *external, not with a competitor.* This may involve an organisation in your own industry that is not a direct competitor or a similar process or product in a different industry. It might also concern a different process or product in a different industry. This may seem pointless but, in fact, by keeping your eye open for good practice elsewhere you might get new ideas for your own organisation.

You will find it helpful to consider the following six steps of benchmarking:

1   Define the process or aspect of your performance that you are comparing.
2   Draw a flow chart of the process.
3   Establish measures.

4   Identify whom to benchmark.

5   Collect data.

6   Determine the gap.

1. Define the process

This is where we choose which aspect of our performance to compare. It will probably be one of your main production or operations processes, and it will be chosen because you have a general dissatisfaction with it or a suspicion that it is an area in which you are falling down.

2. Draw a flow chart of the process

We saw how to do this in Chapter 5.

3. Establish measures

These will be measures of such areas as productivity and quality that are giving you cause for concern. Typically, therefore, against each stage in the flow chart of the process you will note what data you are interested in collecting, such as time to carry out that stage; the amount of waste in that part of the process; the number of times items are sent back for checking or rework; length of delays; the number of items that seem just to go missing; time taken for product or staff to travel from one part or stage of the process to another. As described in Chapter 5, a tongue-in-cheek flow chart might be quite helpful here!

4. Identify whom to benchmark

Remembering the three categories of benchmark organisations – internal, external competitor, external not competitor – you now have to decide whom to use as benchmarks. It may be obvious where to go for your comparisons and so this may be quite a simple decision. If not, you will probably get some ideas from such sources as journals, magazines, newspapers, conferences, and even radio or television programmes. Other likely sources include research reports and industry or government studies of good practice. Do not forget the possible benefits of looking outside your own industry for particularly good examples. You may also consider giving this part of the process over to specialists – benchmarking consultants.

5. Collect data

The nature of the data you will collect will depend on your relationship with the benchmark organisation. If this is distant, or indeed hostile (as might be the case with a competitor), the data may be restricted to what you can obtain from published sources. On the other hand, with say, an internal benchmark or a company in a different industry, you may well be able to strike up a mutually helpful relationship, each of you providing the other with useful information.

If you are able to visit the benchmark, you will have an opportunity to talk with people, use questionnaires, examine records, and observe what is going on. All of this will help to provide not only quantitative data but also qualitative information about how others do things, what methods are used, and what training is provided. Such a visit can be very fruitful.

6. Determine the gap

At its simplest level, 'the gap' will be the difference between your performance in the various measures that you previously identified and that of your benchmark. You may also have been able to compare your way of doing things – your methods, processes, and so on – with theirs, and hence identify a 'qualitative gap'.

Once the gaps are clear, you can then go into the rest of the improvement analysis process – in particular steps 3 to 6 in Chapter 5 (see pages 92 to 106).

Using feedback from others

Who are the significant 'others' who may give your organisation useful feedback? Customers, clearly, form an important group. You may also obtain valuable information about yourself from suppliers, partners in joint ventures, your trade or industry association, government departments, the local authority, and others in what might be called your local environment, such as other businesses, residents' associations, and interest groups.

Customer and supplier surveys

You may choose to use professional survey consultancies. Alternatively you might wish to design and carry out your own survey. We suggest three main approaches to doing this:

- face-to-face interviews with, say, customers, either individually or in what are often referred to as focus groups
- telephone interviews
- questionnaires.

Whatever the approach, you will need to prepare very carefully. The following steps provide a useful guide.

1. Identify your sample

There are some situations in which you can survey 100 per cent of the focus population, but usually you will have to try to find a cross-section that you feel reflects them reasonably well. On other occasions you may deliberately choose a sample that does not attempt to represent the whole population but forms a particularly important subset. For example, suppose you are doing a customer survey: rather than working with all your customers, or with a carefully representative subgroup, you might deliberately focus on your key customers – those who contribute most to your overall sales or profits. The Pareto analysis rule (Chapter 5) may help here – draw a chart of customers and sales for each customer, and pick out the main ones. Alternatively – or additionally – you might concentrate on customers you have recently lost, either those who used to deal with you but now do not, or others with whom you have tried but failed to get contracts.

2. Decide your survey method

Are you going to use interviews (telephone, one-to-one, or focus group), questionnaires, or some combination of them?

3. Determine the information you will require

This may start in a quite general form, eg 'What do you look for in a good supplier?' Later on, you might focus more on suppliers' views of your own organisation, eg 'How well do we meet that requirement?' Questions that probe further can also be used in order to elicit more detailed explanations of what respondents mean, why they say what they are saying, and to request specific examples.

It is often valuable to include questions that compare you with your competitors, or with other well-known exemplars of good practice (either identified by yourself or by the respondent). These questions may be qualitative or may require respondents to rank you against the others.

4. Write to the sample members

This is important – to explain what you are doing, its purpose, and what you will be asking of the sample members.

5. Carry out the survey

6. Analyse results and draw conclusions

Usually this will be the starting-point for other investigations within your organisation, focusing on groups or individuals or both.

Clearly these six steps can be used, with detailed modifications, with suppliers rather than customers.

Using internal feedback (from the organisation itself)

Some of the customer and supplier methods already described apply equally well to internal customers and suppliers, and so may be adapted for internal use.

Another common method used here is the attitude (or opinion) survey.

Attitude Surveys

Attitude (or opinion) surveys have been used for many years within organisations as health checks. Unfortunately the analogy has been all too realistic, the 'patient' seeing the health-check as the end-point rather than taking action to fix the issues it raises. However, increased management attention to the use of quality data, widening availability of IT and analytical support, and recognition of the need for feedback within all processes have led to a step change in how such surveys are used. They are now seen as strategic tools within the contexts of organisational development, change management, and business process enhancement. For example, United Distillers, part of the Guinness Group, uses attitude surveys as a key element in its management portfolio. In so doing it is guided by the following principles:

1. Identify the issues to survey

The business vision, values, strategy, and plans are here examined to identify those behaviours that should characterise the organisation. Senior staff are interviewed to identify issues on which they perceive a need for further information. Staff are consulted, through focus groups, to identify the issues they feel a need to comment on. The output is an agreed framework of issues that:

■ is linked to the business plans

■ significant people want to hear about

■ significant numbers of people want to express views on.

2. Devise the communication strategy

If the data is to be of value, then those completing the survey need fully to understand its importance and how important it is for them to complete the form intelligently. They need to be clear about what will or may happen to the data and what will not be done with it. It is particularly important to address confidentiality issues at this stage.

3. Plan the methodology

Issues here include the choice of survey group (all or sample), type of questionnaire, briefing method, whether or not to impose a restricted time in which to complete the questionnaire, what scales to use, the method by which the questionnaire will be returned for scoring, use of importance and performance scales (see the example on the learning climate survey later in this chapter), and any request for narrative (that is, open-ended), descriptive answers.

4. Collect data

Most surveys are still conducted using paper-based questionnaires, but the use of group-voting technology is increasingly popular.

5. Analyse

Data-analysis options depend on the question and on the questionnaire design. Simple statistics are always useful (eg high and low performance items). However, analysis of interacting factors can also reveal interesting and useful results, for example looking at high-importance yet low-performance items. Correlations between items can also be worth investigating, as can analyses by biodata (eg did the German-speaking rate differently from the French-speaking, or how do men's scores compare with women's?).

6. Carry out a qualitative survey

The data from questionnaire-based surveys does not always

make immediate sense. It is frequently helpful to conduct some form of qualitative survey after the main survey to help fully understand the data. Such processes (eg focus groups) can add a new twist to the data and open up ideas for solutions.

7. Interpret the data

The data collected by such surveys is not in itself diagnostic. It is simply a statement of how the respondents see their reality. Interpretation is therefore very important. For example, does a high score on perceived customer service tell us that we:

∎ are good at delivering the service?
∎ have a real problem if we wish to persuade people that we need to drive up service levels?

This information alone is not sufficient for us to know. We need to interpret the data in the context of the group who provided it, and we need to look for consistencies – and inconsistencies – across the data.

8. Integrate the data into business processes

We have to feed the cumulative results of people's input back to them. However, far more importantly, we need to ensure that the data is not seen as an 'extra'. The data is part of management information and should be used as such: a source of quality feedback to help management tune performance. In most organisations a process for doing this will need to be put in place.

9. Feed back the data to those who provided it

We must acknowledge the efforts of those who provide feedback, help them to see its value, and gain their commitment to future surveys and actions. Usually, local data is more interesting to people, although they may also wish to hear about the wider issues.

10. Analyse the data

Survey data has potential value long after its completion. A sound process enables individuals to analyse the data to obtain further information.

11. Follow-through

Surveys affect organisations only if the planned action takes place. Follow-through needs therefore to be an integral part of the process. Ideally, action plans get incorporated into normal business processes and follow-through occurs there. If not, then complementary processes need to be put in place to gain the return.

12. Evaluate and refine the survey

Any survey is only as good as the previous one. If you want to be able to undertake some tracking or benchmarking, then a substantial part of any survey should be retained when running it again. However, each survey must address current needs, and these change continuously. Part of the process should, therefore, include an evaluation of the last survey: which questions worked well, which provided little value, which still apply, which are now out of date?

Organisational learning climate survey

For trainers and HR specialists a particularly helpful form of internal survey is the organisational learning climate survey. The modes of learning model (Chapter 1, pages 9–14) forms the basis of useful feedback about the learning climate. Working with focus groups (ie reflecting membership of the organisation as a whole), a relatively simple process is as follows (it assumes you have already spent some time explaining the modes to those taking part):

Step 1   Having explained and explored the nature of the modes, ask group members to score each mode on the following scale:

(a) How important is each mode for the future success of your organisation (or for it to be competitive; or for it to achieve its vision; or whatever focus you want to give)?

Score on a scale of 1 to 6, where 1 = not at all important and 6 = vital. We shall refer to this as *importance*.

(b) Once again on a scale of 1 to 6, ask members to score how well each thinks the organisation currently enables people to learn and work in that mode – by the way it designs and implements training, is structured, runs meetings, rewards people, and so on. We shall call this *performance*.

Normally when using this method we find it helpful to ask participants to talk with one another to spark off ideas and share opinions, but nonetheless each person is asked to come up with his or her personal score or (in other words) his or her perception of the learning climate.

Step 2   Prepare a flip chart like that in Table 13 on page 120.

Step 3   Starting with mode 1, ask all those who scored it 1 on importance to put up their hands. Count and enter them on the flip chart. Then do the same with 2 , 3, and so on. Repeat this procedure for mode 1 – performance, and then for all the other modes.

An example from an insurance company is shown in Table 14 on page 121. The numbers of people for each score are shown in bold italics.

Table 13

FLIP CHART FOR MODES OF LEARNING CLIMATE SURVEY

Mode	Importance		Performance		Ratio	Rank of gap
1	1	4	1	4		
	2	5	2	5		
	3	6	3	6		
	Average =		Average =			
2	1	4	1	4		
	2	5	2	5		
	3	6	3	6		
	Average =		Average =			
3	1	4	1	4		
	2	5	2	5		
	3	6	3	6		
	Average =		Average =			
4	1	4	1	4		
	2	5	2	5		
	3	6	3	6		
	Average =		Average =			
5	1	4	1	4		
	2	5	2	5		
	3	6	3	6		
	Average =		Average =			
6	1	4	1	4		
	2	5	2	5		
	3	6	3	6		
	Average =		Average =			
7	1	4	1	4		
	2	5	2	5		
	3	6	3	6		
	Average =		Average =			

Table 14

EXAMPLE OF DATA FOR MODES OF LEARNING CLIMATE SURVEY

Mode	Importance				Performance				Ratio	Rank of gap
1	1 *3*		4 *3*		1 *2*		4 *6*			
	2 *4*		5 *2*		2 *2*		5 *2*			
	3 *5*		6 *1*		3 *5*		6 *1*			
	Average = 3.00				Average = 3.39				1.13	7
2	1 *2*		4 *3*		1 *2*		4 *4*			
	2 *4*		5 *3*		2 *4*		5 *3*			
	3 *3*		6 *3*		3 *5*		6 *0*			
	Average = 3.56				Average = 3.11				0.87	6
3	1 *2*		4 *5*		1 *2*		4 *5*			
	2 *2*		5 *3*		2 *5*		5 *1*			
	3 *2*		6 *2*		3 *5*		6 *0*			
	Average = 3.61				Average = 2.89				0.80	5
4	1 *1*		4 *6*		1 *3*		4 *3*			
	2 *3*		5 *4*		2 *4*		5 *1*			
	3 *3*		6 *2*		3 *7*		6 *0*			
	Average = 3.72				Average = 2.72				0.73	3
5	1 *0*		4 *5*		1 *4*		4 *3*			
	2 *0*		5 *7*		2 *5*		5 *0*			
	3 *1*		6 *5*		3 *6*		6 *0*			
	Average = 4.89				Average = 2.44				0.50	1
6	1 *0*		4 *7*		1 *4*		4 *4*			
	2 *1*		5 *4*		2 *4*		5 *2*			
	3 *3*		6 *3*		3 *4*		6 *0*			
	Average = 4.28				Average = 2.78				0.65	2
7	1 *0*		4 *8*		1 *2*		4 *3*			
	2 *2*		5 *1*		2 *4*		5 *0*			
	3 *6*		6 *1*		3 *9*		6 *0*			
	Average = 3.61				Average = 2.72				0.75	4

Step 4   Also in Table 14 is the average score for each mode on importance and performance. This is calculated as follows, using mode 1 (importance) as an example:

$$\text{average} = \frac{(1 \times 3 + 2 \times 4 + 3 \times 5 + 4 \times 3 + 5 \times 2 + 6 \times 1)}{\text{number of people}}$$

$$= \frac{3 + 8 + 15 + 12 + 10 + 6}{3 + 4 + 5 + 3 + 2 + 1}$$

$$= \frac{54}{18} = 3.00$$

Step 5   Now, for each mode, calculate the ratio between performance and importance. In the example, for mode 1, the ratio is:

$$\frac{\text{average performance score}}{\text{average importance score}}$$

$$= \frac{3.39}{3.00} = 1.13$$

For mode 2 the ratio is $\frac{3.11}{3.56} = 0.87$

and so on. These ratios are shown in Table 14.

Step 6   Now rank the ratios just calculated, with the *lowest* ratio being ranked first, the *highest* seventh. These ranks are shown in Table 14 ('rank of gap'). From this it can be seen that the worst (lowest) ratio of performance to importance is that of mode 5. In other words, Mode 5 is where there is the biggest shortfall between how we think things should be and how we think they are. Mode 6 is second, mode 4 third, and so on.

You will see that mode 1 has a ratio of 1.13 – greater than 1.00. This means that the performance is rated greater than the importance, an implication that perhaps we put *too much* effort into encouraging people to learn and work at mode 1.

It is sometimes helpful to draw graphs of these scores, as in Figures 33 and 34.

This method works well with groups of up to about 40. After that, and particularly when you want to get the perceptions of different subgroups within the organisation, it is better to use commercially available software-based questionnaires designed specifically for this purpose.

Figure 33

PERFORMANCE/IMPORTANCE OF MODES
(data from Table 14)

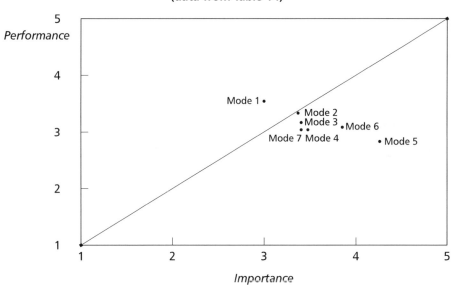

Figure 34

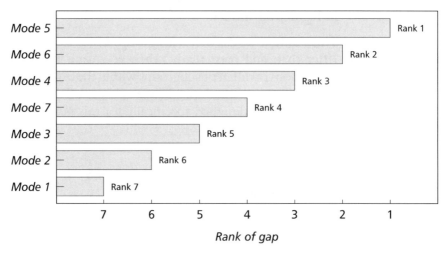

RANK ORDER OF MODES PERFORMANCE/IMPORTANCE GAP
(data from Table 14)

In brief

The identification of organisational training needs is a major focus of our ITN analysis and practice. We have therefore divided the topic into two chapters – Chapter 6 focusing on organisational needs at implementing and improving levels (returning to the performance and learning framework upon which the book is based), and Chapter 7, concentrating on organisational needs at the innovating level.

So in this chapter we have addressed issues of meeting current performance objectives and raising these to new levels, ie implementing and improving. To establish a sound basis for ITN at these levels we have returned to the subject of identifying and using objective data to ensure that our assessment and judgement are based on a good foundation.

As well as reminding ourselves of techniques for obtaining objective data covered in previous chapters we have introduced some new ones:

- benchmarking, to compare performance over a wide range of other organisations or other parts of your own organisation (six steps of benchmarking have been outlined in the form of a manageable procedure to follow)

- customer and supplier surveys, with four main approaches ranging from face- to-face interviews to questionnaires (again following a systematic procedure will ensure the effectiveness and usefulness of this approach)

- organisational learning climate surveys (under the heading of internal feedback) using the modes framework (a six-step sequence has been described in a form that should enable immediate use in situations considered appropriate for this kind of treatment).

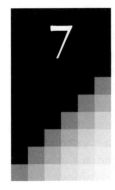

Focusing on Organisational Needs at the Innovating Level

As you will remember from Chapter 1, here we are primarily dealing with changing purposes, objectives, and strategies (see the shaded box in Table 15). We are faced with making strategic decisions about what we do, why, and with whom.

Table 15

FOCUS OF CHAPTER 7

Level of business benefit \ Area of need	Organisational	Group	Individual
I₁: Implementing – doing things well	Meeting current organisational objectives	Working together to meet existing targets and standards	Being competent at the level of existing requirements
I₂: Improving – doing things better	Setting higher objectives and reaching them	Continuous improvement teams	Having and using systematic, continuous improvement skills and processes
I₃: Innovating – doing new and better things	Changing objectives and strategies	Working across boundaries to create new relationships and new products and services	Being able to work differently and more creatively with a shared sense of purpose

At this level many of the issues we identify will, by their very nature, concern strategic changes. Can these be said to be 'training needs'? In the old-fashioned sense of being resolved through direct training or instruction, the answer is probably 'no'. But by now we hope it is clear that we see a much wider role for trainers – as internal consultants facilitating organisational learning.

This view is in line with a recent study published by the Personnel Standards Lead Body (PSLB). Its main conclusions, based on a survey of over 900 senior managers, directors, and chairmen across all sectors, was that personnel functions are not delivering on things of organisational importance, and should take a more strategic role in future. The issues addressed in this chapter, therefore, should be seen in that light: they are about organisational learning. In addition, of course, such strategic changes will usually lead to more conventional training needs further down the line.

Assessing an organisation's development phases

An excellent model for understanding the overall development of an organisation is one that sees it as evolving through a number of phases, as summarised in Table 16 (on page 128). In detail, the phases are as follows:

Pioneer

An individual (occasionally a small group) sees a need or an opportunity, and forms an organisation to capitalise on the opportunity or to meet the need.

The essence of the pioneer organisation is looseness and informality. Everything revolves around the pioneer themselves hence the flat or even 'spider's-web' structure. There are virtually no formal systems or processes; rather, everything is done on an *ad hoc* basis. It is no surprise, therefore, that there tends to be very little formal training – or ITN – in this type of organisation.

Phase:	Pioneer	Overripe pioneer	Rational	Bureaucratic	Shake-up	Integrated
	Individual Idea Energy/drive Direction Enthusiasm Informality Flexibility	Chaos Complexity Confusion Exploitation	Formality Systems Specialisation Functions Professionalisation Order Quality assurance	Rigidity Compartments Conflicts Poor communications Inward-looking Separation	Loosening Re-organisation Attitude surveys Continuous improvement Customer care Excellence Re-engineering	Individuals/teams; department; inner/outer; ideas TQM Lean manufacturing Learning company
Structure:	*spider's web* *flat*	*falling apart*	*pyramid*	*hierarchy*	*matrix*	*energy flow* *clover leaf*
Processes:	Ad hoc	Uncontrolled	Systematic Differentiated Under control	Proceduralised	Customer-focused Continuous improvement	Energy flow Synergistic Systemic
Relationships:	Leader–follower Owner–manager Power-based	Master–servant Exploitative	Manager-managed Role-based Diversity: minimised	Boss–subordinate	Team leader–team membership Customer–supplier Collaborative Diversity: accepted	Networking Leadership Diversity: needed, wanted, valued Membership Dialogue
Identify:	Pioneer-centred	Power-dominated	'Technology'-driven	Bureaucracy-based	Customer-focused Market-led	Associative Partnership
Integration:	Individual ego	Disintegration – becoming free	System	Welded	Activity Movement Turbulence	Flow

Table 16

SUMMARY OF AN ORGANISATION'S DEVELOPMENT PHASES

Overripe Pioneer After a time, the informality that is the essence of the pioneer phase starts to become a serious problem. Things become too loose, chaotic, and uncontrolled. Employees feel unprotected from the personal whims of the pioneer. There is a strongly felt need for order, rationality, and stability.

Sometimes, too, there is a succession crisis when the original pioneer retires, moves on, or dies. Who is to take over? Very often the family heir does not have the intuitive flair of the original pioneer.

Moving on to the next phases presents a real challenge to pioneers. Some sell up and either retire or, quite probably, set up a new pioneer organisation. Alternatively, if the founder-owner is going to remain with the organisation while it moves through the succeeding phases, he or she will have to learn to adopt quite different roles – what Mike Pedler and Ian Anderson have described as moving from owner-operator to owner-manager to owner-director to owner-developer.

Rational The desire for rationality is realised in this phase. Relationships become based on formally defined roles and job descriptions. Processes are codified and written down. Everybody knows where they fit in, what they are expected to do, and how to do it in increasingly specialised or differentiated departments and units. Employees are protected by contracts and agreements. In the rational phase we find much evidence of systematic training – including ITN – for individuals, groups and the organisation as a whole. This is where many of the I_1 (implementing) approaches are used. Competence frameworks, appraisal, surveys, all fit in well with the overall ethos of rationality. Much training is off-the-job, with emphasis on courses and instruction.

Bureaucratic Here we are using the term 'bureaucratic' with its present-day negative connotations. The pendulum has swung too far again, this time towards rationality and order, which have led to rigidity, poor communications, and an excessively hierarchical orientation. There is an increasingly inwards focus, with energy sapped by constant attention to maintaining existing procedures and dealing with conflicts arising from fierce compartmentalisation.

Shake-up   Once the rigidity of the bureaucratic phase has been recognised, it is time to try to loosen up again. Many different forms of loosening may be experimented with, including matrix structures, teambuilding, attitude surveys, customer care programmes, process re-engineering, and, of course, reorganisation after reorganisation after... These initiatives tend to remain driven by a mindset that is still basically hierarchical and can sometimes more resemble nostalgia for the pioneering phase than eagerness for integration. For those involved, this phase may seem rather positive and exciting, or unstable and threatening, or yet another example of numerous change programmes that come to nought. (As stated before, research shows that 75 per cent of such programmes fail or are abandoned within three years!) The challenge is to make this a bridge for moving forwards rather than a never-ending cycle of 'this is it' change programmes – the chaos that Tom Peters thrives on, but that wears others out!

Here we should expect to find the I_2 (improving) approach to training and ITN: more sophisticated appraisal systems, such as 360° feedback, team development, customer surveys, benchmarking, working with continuous improvement tools, and learning on-the-job on 'real-life' projects.

Integrated   This is where the needs of both the individual and the whole are met, where small units feel both independent *and* part of a larger whole. An organisation that has moved from hierarchy to markets and networks, where the *leader* as an individual or role with formal power over followers is replaced by *leadership*, is in a process of 'meaning-making in a community of practice' (Drath and Palus 1994).

A number of approaches is being advocated for helping movement into this integrated phase. In general, each approach has been born out of a particular stream of expertise. Thus we have total quality management (TQM, from statistics and engineering); lean manufacturing (from production engineering); the learning organisation (Peter Senge, from systems thinking); and the learning company (Pedler and colleagues, from learning and development). One of the challenges facing these streams is how they can integrate with, and learn from, one another.

To help move towards the integrated phase we use the I_3 (innovating) approaches described in this book, such as seven beacons, dialogue, role negotiation, customer-mapping, U-procedure, and indeed an understanding of where we are in terms of the phases model.

A picture of where your organisation is in terms of these phases can help you to decide which approach to ITN is likely to be needed. Indeed, in broad terms we can map the phases onto the three levels of learning:

Pioneer   focuses mainly on I_1 (implementing). Most people learn to work in modes 1 to 4.

Overripe pioneer slips back a bit.

Rational   focuses again on I_1 (implementing). Now most people learn and work in modes 1 to 3, with a select few in mode 5 (deciding what the others should do).

Bureaucratic   the organisation will tend to remain stuck at I_1.

Shake-up   now does I_2 (improving), as well as I_1 (implementing). Many people now learn and work in modes 1 to 5.

Integrated   works at all three levels: implementing, improving and innovating. People work in modes 1 to 7.

As well as HR specialists, line managers also relate very

readily to this model. It helps explain what is going on, and what development issues the organisation – and hence the people in it – are faced with.

Diagnosis of your organisation's phase

In fact most organisations contain elements of each phase; also, different departments or units might be in quite different phases from others – which often gives rise to tension, conflicts, and other difficulties.

One simple way to ask people to make a diagnosis is to describe the phases and then ask people to distribute 100 points across them, according to their perception of the organisation's development. You can then tabulate these as shown in Table 17.

Table 17

EXAMPLE DATA FOR DIAGNOSIS OF AN ORGANISATION'S DEVELOPMENT PHASE

	% in each phase as seen by person							Total	Average
	A	B	C	D	E	F	G		
Pioneer	5	0	0	30	0	0	10	45	6.43
Overripe pioneer	0	0	5	10	0	0	5	20	2.86
Rational	20	10	5	30	0	10	30	105	15.00
Bureaucratic	30	40	60	30	30	30	30	250	35.71
Shake-up	40	40	20	0	70	40	20	230	32.86
Integrated	5	10	10	0	0	20	5	50	7.14
Total	100	100	100	100	100	100	100	700	100.00

(Check: overall total should equal 100 × number of people,
ie 100 × 7 = 700. It does!)

This profile can then be plotted, as in Figure 35, which shows the consensus view. However, the figures show that person D clearly sees much more of a pioneer element than do the others. It would be important to talk about this – to understand why D has this view.

Figure 35

PROFILE OF AN ORGANISATION'S DEVELOPMENT PHASES

Data from Table 17

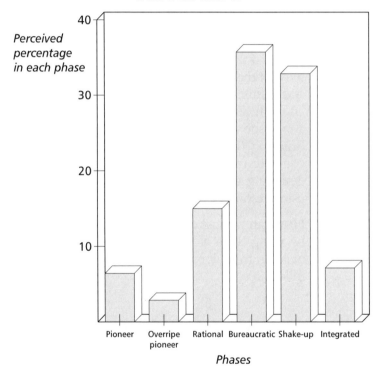

Using the 'seven beacons' of the successful organisation

The phases model gives a useful overall picture of the organisation and its next developmental challenge. This now needs to be worked on in more detail.

The *seven beacons*, an idea that originates from the Netherlands, helps with this more detailed process. These are the 'beacons of success', ie the seven main elements that need to be considered:

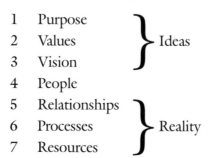

1   Purpose
2   Values   } Ideas
3   Vision
4   People
5   Relationships
6   Processes   } Reality
7   Resources

It will be seen that 'people' lie at the division between *ideas* and *reality*. Thus, on the one hand, people 'have' a sense of the purpose of the organisation, decide the values, and picture the vision. These in a way are all abstractions 'in the heads' of the people. At the same time, people are also responsible for translating these ideas into reality: bringing the abstract purpose, values and vision into concrete reality by creating organisational conditions, designing and implementing processes, and obtaining and using resources.

How can you use these beacons for diagnosis? You do so by using them as a basis for exploration and decision-making. In so doing, you can work with 'people' twice, as follows.

Step 1:
People – now.   What are the characteristics of the people in our organisation? How many do we have? What are their strengths? Weaknesses? Competencies? Which of the seven modes are they able to work in? What are their hopes, fears, aspirations? What diversity do we have in terms of gender, race, abilities, age?

Step 2: Purpose.   What is our purpose or mission? A lot of organisations these days produce 'mission statements' that are really, in all honesty, pretty shallow – 'To be the best saddlemaker's bottom-knocker producer in the South-East', for example.

Although being the best in your sector might be a useful thing to strive for, is it a real *purpose* as such? We prefer an approach that tackles such questions as:

> 'In what way would the world (or the South-East, or the industry, or whatever) be worse off if our organisation were not here – if it disappeared overnight?'

Imaginative techniques can also be helpful. Here is one, on similar lines to the above:

> Imagine your organisation as a human being who has just died. What would an obituary say of it, outlining its overall life history and achievements or contributions to the world?
>
> How do you feel about this organisational obituary? What would you really like it to be able to say?

The aim here is to try to get a more meaningful sense of purpose, of what your organisation stands for, than many of the mission statements that adorn annual reports and plush reception areas.

Step 3: Values. An organisation's values underpin the way it does things. In fact it will always have two sets of these:

■ espoused values, ie those it claims to hold, in the form of statements, slogans, and formal policies of 'the way we do things'

■ values-in-use, ie those actually lived out, as expressed in 'the way things are really done'.

Very often there is a gap between espoused values and values-in-use. For example, many organisations claim to value diversity and have equal opportunities policies written and distributed to staff. But observation of what actually happens might find, say, that:

■ 70 per cent of supervisor staff or below are women,

whereas 90 per cent of senior staff are men

■ 2 per cent of employees are black or Asian, and all of these in non-managerial grades

■ access to the premises is impossible in a wheelchair

■ the employee handbook contains a number of cartoon illustrations, all showing white men in managerial positions and white women in process-worker jobs.

> A useful exercise is to go through all your documents, procedures, and physical resources such as buildings, access points, offices, car parks, canteens, and so on, and look at what subtle, hidden messages about values-in-use they are conveying.
>
> Another way to get at values-in-use is to examine an unsatisfactory incident, where something happened that caused a conflict, led to a dispute, or left a number of people feeling unhappy, let down, frustrated, angry, or whatever. Really probe into the incident – not with the intention of seeing who was to blame, but rather to see what clash of values was involved and therefore what, in practice, the ruling values are.

A major transport undertaking espoused values of openness and equality of opportunity with written policy statements.

A young Afro-Caribbean man was interviewed for a job and was told he could not apply to be a driver because it was thought he would have problems handling the racism in the depot.

Management was thereby not only acknowledging that the company did not value equal opportunity in practice, but were also colluding with racism by taking no steps to prevent it or to help individuals to challenge it.

In practice the ruling values are often about power,

authority, who gets the last word, who gets listened to, who gets scapegoated, who is accepted or marginalised, what happens to ethical issues, and so on. You may well also find other clusters of values-in-use in your own organisation.

Once you have identified espoused values and values-in-use, you will then be in a position to look at the gap between these and decide what needs doing to close it.

Step 4: Vision. Some people use the word 'vision' for what we have termed 'mission'. For us, vision refers to a picture of how we want things to be by a certain date – say one, two or three years from now. This picture needs to be quite detailed, in terms of providing replies to such questions as:

- What will our organisation be doing then? How will this show itself? How will people notice?

- Who will our customers, suppliers, and other stakeholders be? What will be their experience of us? What will they be saying about us?

- What will newspaper reports, trade journal articles, and radio or TV programmes be saying about us?

Try to make this picture rich in imaginative detail: flesh it out. Consider actually drawing it, as well as (or instead of) creating a word-picture.

Step 5: Relationships. Now we start to make plans for converting these ideas into reality. Here we are referring to relationships between various individuals, groups, departments, units and functions, as well as relationships between ourselves and our suppliers, customers, workforce, and other stakeholders. How are these relationships at present? How do they need to be if we are to achieve our vision? What do we need to change?

Here, of course, we may need to gain insight by collecting information about how these relationships are using some of the methods described in Chapters 6 and 8.

Step 6: Processes. The way our processes work is in part a reflection of our values-in-use. So if we have a process that produces numerous errors and customer complaints, a value-in-use is that it is OK to let down the customer and then to spend energy handling complaints, no matter what our customer care policy claims. Or, if we have recruitment procedures that consistently provide us only with men, then our values-in-use are not consistent with our espoused values of equal opportunity.

> A major civil engineering contractor was concerned about shortage of recruits. It therefore decided to make a real effort to recruit women into various design office jobs that, until then, had been held almost entirely by men. Putting this policy into action involved:
>
> ▪ visiting local schools and talking to groups of girls
> ▪ encouraging the contractor's own clerical staff to apply for retraining for technical posts
> ▪ running open days and meetings to enable women to get a feel of what the work might involve
> ▪ encouraging job-sharing
> ▪ advertising for women returners to become trainees
> ▪ establishing crèche facilities
> ▪ moving to flexible working hours.

Here the espoused value of equal opportunity was translated into reality by the considerable efforts made to recruit women. So we are concerned here with looking at our processes, procedures, systems, and ways of doing things, and checking to what extent they reflect the values-in-use that we want.

Step 7: Resources. This mainly refers to physical resources, but also to finance. To achieve our vision, in a way consistent with our desired values-in-use, what resources shall we need and how shall we finance them?

Step 8: People –
from now on.   Finally, we come back to people. Given our pictures and decisions about mission, values, vision, relationships, processes, and resources, what sort of people do we want? How many? Where? How do we want them to be – in terms of modes, competencies, diversity, health, morale, age, and so on? Comparing this with the picture of our people as they are right now (step 1), what are we going to have to change? How will we do this?

Environmental audit

A particular type of survey, involving many forms of data and working at I_1, I_2, or I_3 levels (or indeed at all three), is the environmental audit. As its name suggests, this aims at finding out what you are doing to your environment and, in a sense, what it thinks of you. Typically it will involve the following:

1   Be sure you know why you are doing the survey. Is it to ensure you do not run into legal trouble or get bad publicity? Or do you want to go further, and make a real contribution to environmental improvement?

2   Select areas to be investigated, such as emissions of solids, liquids, gases, noise, light (into air, water, or land); storage issues; site management; and transportation congestion.

3   Check existing standards, either statutory requirements or regulatory guidelines.

4   Collect your data by means of objective measures, visits, interviews, and focus-group meetings.

Organisations that are really interested in ecological issues go a lot further, doing an environmental track not only of their direct processes but also of those of their suppliers of raw materials and components.

This process, developed jointly by Volvo, the Swedish Environmental Research Institute, and the Swedish

Federation of Industries calculates an 'environmental index' for every component in a finished product (such as a car). The environmental index typically involves considering six factors:

∎ biodiversity
∎ health
∎ production
∎ resources
∎ aesthetic values.

These are calculated for three principal phases of the overall component life-cycle:

∎ production
∎ use
∎ destruction.

The final decision on raw materials, methods, component design, and so on takes the overall environmental index into account.

General Motors might have been well advised to carry out an environmental audit when, in 1990, buyers of Cadillacs complained that their prestigious vehicles stalled at low speeds. An I_1 (implementing) solution was carried out by installing a new computer chip that allowed a richer mixture of fuel and air into the engine. Stalling was removed but, unfortunately, because the engineers had not been thinking holistically, three times as much carbon monoxide was now being pumped into the atmosphere – a fact that was evidently not considered important.

As a consequence, in 1995 General Motors had to recall 500,000 cars, at a cost of $30 million. On top of this they were fined $11 million and agreed to spend a further $8 million on a form of community environmental service, such as buying old, polluting cars and taking them off the road.

Large-systems interventions

Traditionally, work at a strategic level is done by senior managers or board members on behalf of the organisation. More recently, however, a number of approaches known generically as large-systems interventions has been gaining in popularity. In principle these bring together in large groups people seen as reflecting all the organisation's stakeholders – employees, owners, customers, suppliers, and neighbours. They use methods such as those described in this chapter or, often, similar processes specifically designed for the purpose (see, for example, Weisbord 1992) to 'discover common ground', map out a *shared* picture of the future, and then make separate action plans for their own role in moving forward.

This approach, often known as future search, is used not only in industry but also in the public sector, the health service, and voluntary organisations.

> In Sheffield a future search conference was held, bringing together people from the council, health, transport, education, business, commerce, police, media, and voluntary services, and 'ordinary citizens', and creating a network of future leaders from these various stakeholder groups so that they could work individually, yet together, on developing the city over the next generation.

Attwood, Pedler and Wilkinson (1993) describe five key ideas for successful large systems interventions:

Key 1 'Getting the whole organisation into the room together'

The first principle is that anyone who will be affected by a change should also be an architect of it. 'Getting everyone in the room together' happens in two ways:

▮ As part of a diagnostic process, data is collected from all parts of the organisation, including the views of users, customers, and other stakeholders.

▋ Decisions are made in meetings of representatives of all organisation members and stakeholders. (In a small organisation this might mean literally everybody; in a larger one, representation will be necessary.)

Key 2 Public Learning

Whole-system development derives its power from public evidence of learning and commitment from 'everyone in the room'. People hear colleagues and stakeholders from other departments, agencies, and locations make action plans to change relationships; everyone sees the senior management team questioned on their policies and receiving feedback, which often leads to changed direction.

This needs effective preparation by a number of teams, including a leadership team of the chief executives and senior officers, in order to give overall leadership and direction to the change; and a development team of representative members, in order to develop the design of the change process; and also a consultants team to guide the change process itself.

Key 3 Diversity

Whole-system development builds in maximum diversity to represent the full complexity of the system. The full range of departments, professional groupings, grades and status, gender, ethnic composition, age, and any other relevant criteria – and also a full array of stakeholders and service users – are included.

Key 4 Effective small-group dynamics

Everybody is represented and has a say, but participants also listen to the views and ideas of others. People work in 'max-mix' (maximum mix) groups so that the diversity of the complex whole is present in the events forming part of the change process. They also work in organisationally-based groups in order to agree actions to deliver the joint agenda.

Key 5 Follow-through

The change process raises high expectations that must be followed through. Continuing support for action and learning is provided to make sure that the new ways of doing business and delivering services are brought to life.

These five key items help us to see what can now be achieved when the intelligence, creativity, and skill of a critical mass of the whole workforce, supported by customers, suppliers, and key stakeholders are freely given to achieve a clearly understood strategic purpose.

This is in stark contrast to the situation in so many organisations, where individuals try to do their best but, somehow, the system as a whole does not seem to work. It gets in the way, with gaps and delays between planning and delivery, and a combination of parochial interests, as well as cynicism about change, frustrating even the best individual efforts.

In brief

Organisational needs at the innovating level are the focus of this chapter. Here we are involved in making strategic decisions about changing purposes and objectives. Again, the role of the trainer comes into question in these areas – requiring internal consultancy and facilitating organisational learning in a broad sense. The techniques considered most useful at this level of learning and performance are:

- assessing needs in terms of the organisation's development phase. Here we have translated a basic phases model into a useable diagnostic tool.

- linking the phases of organisational development to the levels of learning and performance introduced earlier. We think that you will find it valuable to link consideration of training and learning needs to basic models such as these because it will allow for a degree of consistency and integrity in your analysis.

■ the seven beacons of the successful organisation, which enable you to work in more detail on the overall picture of the organisation and its next developmental challenge provided by the phases model. A way of using the beacons for diagnosis is described, using various techniques for working through an eight-step sequence encompassing resources, processes, relationships, vision, values, purpose, and – most importantly – people (examined twice, for good measure).

■ environmental audits – forms of survey that may have their uses at I_1, I_2 or I_3 levels. Some guidelines are provided on how best to use these audits.

■ large-systems interventions.

References

ATTWOOD M, PEDLER M and WILKINSON D *Whole System Development*. Whole System Development, 1995.

DRATH W and PALUS C *Making Common Sense: Leadership as meaning-making in communities of practice*. Greensboro; Centre for Creative Leadership, 1994.

WEISBORD M *Discovering Common Ground*. Berrett-Kohler, 1992.

8

Focusing on
Group Needs

We now turn to the identification of implementing, improving and innovating needs of groups – the shaded area in Table 18.

Table 18

FOCUS OF CHAPTER 8

Area of need / Level of business benefit	Organisational	Group	Individual
I_1: Implementing – doing things well	Meeting current organisational objectives	Working together to meet existing targets and standards	Being competent at the level of existing requirements
I_2: Improving – doing things better	Setting higher objectives and reaching them	Continuous improvement teams	Having and using systematic, continuous improvement skills and processes
I_3: Innovating – doing new and better things	Changing objectives and strategies	Working across boundaries to create new relationships and new products and services	Being able to work differently and more creatively with a shared sense of purpose

We shall start by taking an overall view of the development of a team, using a stage model and linking a number of team competencies to specific stages. We shall then take a number of core team competencies and, labelling these basic team skills, describe a method for analysing members' behaviour, and hence arriving at a diagnostic picture of both the team as a whole and individual members.

Stages of a team's development

Just as organisations move through certain phases (see Chapter 7), so teams or groups go through a number of developmental stages, as shown in Table 19.

Table 19

STAGES OF A TEAM'S DEVELOPMENT

Stages	Issues	Level
0: getting ready	Preparation for new teamworking initiative, taking into account previous experiences, attitudes, and opinions of actual and potential team members	
1: getting started	Launching the team, dealing with basic issues, getting down to what is essential to start working together; identifying areas of concern to be dealt with at stage 2.	I_1: implementing
2: getting going	Sorting out issues, roles, and relationships sufficiently to be able to get the task completed.	
3: getting results	Becoming effective, working well as a task-oriented, businesslike unit; becoming ambitious enough to look for areas of improvement; formulating and implementing improvement plans.	I_2: improving
4: getting together	Learning to co-operate, requiring that any residual relationship issues be addressed and difficulties worked through.	I_3: innovating
5: getting through	Working creatively, generating new solutions, and trying new methods. Team members help one another to become more imaginative and creative.	

There are two other 'stages', which need to be considered separately because they can occur at any time during the development of the team in the five stages just mentioned. These two other stages are:

Stage 6: ending This is when the team closes down. This may be because it has finished its task (eg a project team) or because of reorganisation, a more disruptive reason.

Whichever the reason, a team should spend as much energy and conscious effort on managing its ending as on its forming. This will include acknowledging and celebrating what has been learned, and clearing up any 'unfinished business' either within the team or with external people.

Stage X: getting on with others In some ways one might expect this to occur after the team has learned to get on with itself (stages 1–4 or 5) but experience shows that teams can benefit by making conscious efforts right from the start to develop better working relationships with customers, suppliers, and other teams, internally and externally. This will lead to cross-functional working.

It is often very helpful for a team to take stock of where it is in terms of its profile across these stages – at any given time it is likely to contain elements of most, with one or two predominant. One way to get a measure of this is to use the same technique as for the organisation's phases (Chapter 7, Table 16). Alternatively you might like to try the following method, which is a form of paired comparisons. Whichever you use, it is better not to include stages 6 or X, for, as we have seen, these are additional possibilities at any of the other stages.

Take a series of file cards and write a description of each of the six stages being considered (0–5) on a separate card. Give each team member a set of these six cards and ask him/her to choose any two at random. Next, each team member chooses that one of the two cards that more accurately describes the team as, in his/her opinion, it is at present. Everyone then allocates points to the two cards. The points must total 100.

For example, suppose the two cards chosen at random are stages 3 and 5. I decide that my team is nearer to stage 3 than 5 – quite a bit so. I therefore give 75 points to stage 3 and 25 to stage 5. (NB: If I think that the team is *equally like or unlike both cards*, then I give them 50 points each.)

You enter the scores in Table 20. In this case, look along the left-hand (card pairs) column until you find the row marked 3:5. Then the score you have given to stage 3 (ie 75) goes in the grey cell in the stage 3 column, and 25 points goes in the grey cell in the stage 5 column. So you enter scores only in the shaded cells.

	Stages					
Card pairs	0	1	2	3	4	5
3:4						
3:5				75		25
4:5						

The cards are then shuffled and another pair chosen at random. The process continues until all the shaded cells in the table are filled in. (There are 30 of these – 15 pairs.) When this has been completed, as in the worked example in Table 21, add up each column. These scores can either be drawn on a chart directly or first of all be converted to percentages by being divided by 15 (the number of card pairs) and then plotted. This plot is a profile of the team against all the stages. It sets the context for the identification of team needs, and indeed can give a direct pointer to some of the latter.

Table 20

BLANK PRO FORMA FOR DIAGNOSIS OF PROFILE OF STAGES OF A TEAM'S DEVELOPMENT

Card pairs	Stages						Total
	0	1	2	3	4	5	
0:1							100
0:2							100
0:3							100
0:4							100
0:5							100
1:2							100
1:3							100
1:4							100
1:5							100
2:3							100
2:4							100
2:5							100
3:4							100
3:5							100
4:5							100
Total							1500
% [Total ÷ 15]							100
Rank							

Table 21

WORKED EXAMPLE OF DIAGNOSIS OF PROFILE OF STAGES OF A TEAM'S DEVELOPMENT

Stages

Card pairs	0	1	2	3	4	5	Total
0:1	50	50					100
0:2	00		100				100
0:3	00			100			100
0:4	00				100		100
0:5	00					100	100
1:2		10	090				100
1:3		00		100			100
1:4		00			100		100
1:5		00				100	100
2:3			020	080			100
2:4			030		070		100
2:5			045			055	100
3:4				065	035		100
3:5				075		025	100
4:5					060	040	100
Total	50	60	285	420	365	320	1500
% [Total ÷ 15]	3.33	4.00	19.00	28.00	24.33	21.33	100.00
Rank	6	5	4	1	2	3	

The worked example shows that, for this particular person, the team is primarily in stage 3, with progress up towards stages 4 and 5. Its main developmental task will be to continue that move forwards – making further conscious efforts at learning to co-operate and then to work creatively together.

A separate diagnosis may be useful to ask people how they think the team does at getting on with others (stage X). A process known as role negotiation is helpful for this (described later in this chapter).

When the time for closing down a team arises, it will be helpful to ask members about previous occasions when this has happened, how they handled it, and what they would like to do this time.

Different perceptions of stages of team's development

Sometimes you will find that members differ in their pictures of where the team is. In such cases we usually prepare graphs of each individual's scores and share these, using them as a basis for further conversation and exploration. A simplified example, with just four team members, is shown in Figure 36 (on page 152). You will see that team members A and B have different perceptions from those of C and D.

We shall now describe two other strategic-level diagnostic tools: U-procedure and SWOT analysis.

The U-procedure

U-procedure is a good way of taking a strategic look at a group, department, or indeed the whole organisation, especially if it is fairly small. It involves seven 'biographical' steps taking us from the recent past into the present, and hence forwards to the future (Figure 37 on page 152).

Figure 36

STAGES OF A TEAM'S DEVELOPMENT AS PERCEIVED BY DIFFERENT TEAM MEMBERS

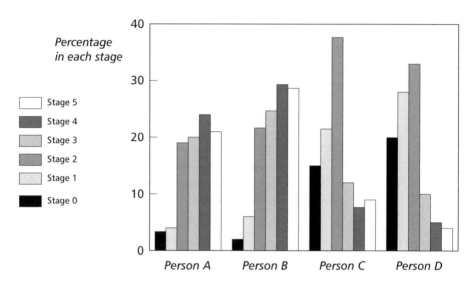

Figure 37

THE U-PROCEDURE

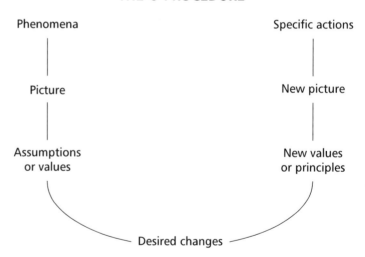

Step 1: What are the phenomena?

This refers to happenings, events, characteristics, the way we do things, the way things are – successes and problems. It is useful to cluster them under headings such as relationships, procedures and processes, resources, image, and quality of work.

Step 2: What is the overall picture?

What do these phenomena tell us about the overall state of the unit, department, or team? Try to summarise this in one or two simple phrases or metaphors, or even perhaps film or TV titles, getting at the essence behind the phenomena: 'stabbing ourselves in the back'; 'one step forwards and three steps sideways'; 'physician, heal thyself!'; 'one foot in the grave'.

Step 3: What assumptions or values lie behind this picture?

Try to arrive at the basic values, beliefs, principles, or assumptions that appear to underlie the picture gained at step 2. Put yourself in the position of an disinterested outsider observing what is going on.

Step 4: Do we want to change, and, if so, why?

Do we really want to change – or would we prefer to hang on to some dysfunctional characteristics that are nonetheless in some way attractive? (Ask yourself what these characteristics are protecting us from – what useful purpose are they serving?)

If we do not change, what will be the consequences? Can we cope with these? If we did not exist, what would be the loss to our market/economy/industry/profession/ society? What is our unit's mission – why are we here?

Step 5: What new values or principles do we now want?

If we are to carry out our mission, what will our core values need to be? Some of these will be the same as in step 3, others will build on those, and others will be actual opposites.

Step 6: What new picture will we get if we introduce these values?

What will they mean for all the people concerned? Should we involve them now in this very process, perhaps revisiting steps 4 and 5? Will it be feasible to implement them? Going back to some of the successes and problems described in step 1, how would they look if these new values and principles were applied to them?

Step 7: What specific actions make sense at this point?

How shall we start to implement the strategy – where shall we begin? We need broad action plans, allowing as much involvement as possible by all concerned.

SWOT analysis

SWOT analysis is a technique widely used by a group, department, unit, or indeed the whole organisation to look at its strategic position. The acronym stands for Strengths, Weaknesses, Opportunities, and Threats. Often presented as a square like that in Figure 38, the information required for each cell can be obtained in a number of ways, including brainstorming, interviewing, surveys, and analysing objective data. Some indicative questions are shown in Figure 38. Clearly you can use others around the same theme.

Figure 38

SWOT ANALYSIS

Strengths	Opportunities
■ What are we good at? ■ What do we do best? ■ What are our assets – finance, plant, equipment, people, information, learning, processes, products, systems, reputation, sales, relationships? ■ How do these compare with others', especially competitors'?	■ What changes do we expect to see over the next five years that will present us with opportunities? ■ What new openings will arise?
Weaknesses	Threats
■ What do we do badly? ■ Where do we let ourselves down? ■ What are our weaknesses – finance, plant, equipment, people, information, learning, processes, products, systems, reputation, sales, relationships? ■ How do these compare with others', especially competitors'?	■ What do other people have that is better than what we have, and what do they do better than us? ■ How easily can others enter into competition with us? ■ What changes are coming that will affect us – in particular, what changes that will present us with problems?

Mainly internal factors

Mainly external factors

Feedback from others

There are a number of ways in which teams or other groups (such as units or departments) can get feedback from others. Here we will consider three:

■ role negotiation

■ customer/supplier- mapping

■ functional audit.

Role negotiation

Role negotiation is a most valuable technique for sharing information between groups of people – or between individuals, for that matter, within a team. Here we shall describe it at the intergroup level.

It is primarily a method of diagnosing the state of a relationship, hence leading to the possibility of further analysis and subsequent action – including training. At the same time it is itself an intervention that, simply by being carried out, can lead to a positive development in the relationship.

The process is simple. Each of the two groups involved thinks about the relationship, and then tells the other group the following:

∎ things you do that we find helpful – please continue with them!

∎ things you do that we find unhelpful – please stop, or at least do fewer of them!

∎ things you do not do that we would find helpful – please start!

Obviously, sharing this information is only the start. What follows is a conversation about the feedback, exploration of the items, checking understanding, and then some agreements and mutual contracting of new behaviours. These contracts are often written up in a record and agreement of the meeting.

In the BICC case described in Chapter 1, role negotiation was used extensively. At one session, team members from the stores department gave feedback to dispatch, and vice versa, as follows:

From dispatch to stores:

Please continue:

∎ supplying drums when required
∎ collecting drums on time
∎ generally being helpful
∎ buying pints after work on a Friday!

Please stop:

∎ encroaching on our patch.

Please start:

∎ covering bins
∎ improving awareness of overhead-crane hazards on cross-walks.

From stores to dispatch:

Please continue:

∎ (sometimes) asking rather than demanding to borrow stacker.

Please stop:

∎ parking finished cable on the road
∎ leaving trailers on the crossing
∎ temporarily dropping drums on the road
∎ (sometimes) demanding rather than asking to borrow stacker.

Please start:

∎ asking rather than demanding.

These points were talked about at some length, and a number of agreements made. In most cases (eg parking finished cable on the road), the 'offending' party recognised that what they were doing was unhelpful but felt so constrained by the limitations of current processes and resources that they could not do otherwise. This led to a joint problem-solving session and a recommendation to management for changing methods, which was implemented.

In the BICC case, agreements were made fairly easily. Roger Harrison, who 'invented' role negotiation, describes a response formula, to be used by the recipient of a request for changes in more difficult situations (Harrison 1995):

++ I/we'll be glad to do it – I didn't realise this was an issue for you.

+ I/we shall do as you request, if you can show how it

contributes to the whole.

0   I am/we are willing to negotiate a fair exchange for what you want.

–   What you ask is very difficult for me/us. I/we suggest we work on something else.

Roger Harrison also describes some of the positive characteristics of role negotiation:

■ It focuses on work relationships – on what people do – using everyday, work-related words and ideas.

■ It avoids probing deep levels of feelings or 'psychoanalysing' the relationship.

■ It helps people to identify and use in a positive way the sources of power and influence available to them.

■ It is highly action-oriented, leading to negotiated agreements, and hence, in practice, to relatively stable and lasting changes.

■ It involves a clear and simple procedure.

Customer- and supplier-mapping

Role negotiation is a fairly open-ended approach to diagnosing intergroup relationships. A more structured approach, specifically intended for examining relationships between a group and its customers or suppliers (internal or external), is provided by customer- and supplier-mapping. We shall start with customer-mapping.

Step 1   Group members identify the main processes that the group or unit carries out. These are entered in column 1 of Table 22 (on page 160).

Step 2   The group then identifies the customers for each process – the recipient(s) of the output from that process. These go in column 2.

| Step 3 | Next the group takes each process in turn and imagines themselves in the position of the various customers. What do they think would satisfy or delight these customers? This goes in column 3. |

| Step 4 | Having identified what would satisfy or delight each customer, the group then uses column 4 to write its opinion of how well it is doing, giving reasons. |

| Step 5 | The last step is in effect a form of the role negotiation that we have just looked at. In this case the group identifies things that: |

(a) the customer does that make it easy to satisfy or delight him/her

(b) the customer does that make it hard to satisfy or delight him/her

(c) the customer does not do that, if he/she did do, would make it easier to satisfy or delight him/her.

| Step 6 | Now the group needs to talk with the various customers, to check out their (the group's) perceptions (columns 3 and 4), and share their role negotiation (column 5). |

| Step 7 | Following step 6, a number of issues will have been identified that can be analysed and worked on, as outlined in Chapter 5. |

Table 23 (on page 161) is for the converse process, ie mapping a group's suppliers. Obviously, a good dialogue process should involve both parties' doing their respective preparation prior to the meeting and talking together.

The functional audit

The functional audit is a particular case of feedback to a group – where the group is a whole function or department within an organisation. It could also be adapted for smaller teams.

Table 22

CUSTOMER MAP

(1)	(2)	(3)	(4)	(5)
Main processes	Customers of the processes	What we think will satisfy or delight the customers	How well we think we are doing at satisfying or delighting these customers	What customers could do/stop doing/start doing to make it easier for us to satisfy or delight customers

Table 23

SUPPLIER MAP

(1)	(2)	(3)	(4)	(5)
Main processes	Suppliers to those processes	What would satisfy or delight us – the suppliers' customers	How well the suppliers are doing at satisfying or delighting us	What we could do/stop doing/ start to do that would make it easier for the suppliers to satisfy or delight us

One way to carry out such an audit would be to use customer-mapping. However, an alternative, more structured process has been devised, and may be explained by means of an example concerning the personnel function.

In 1993 the Personnel Standards Lead Body (PSLB
– now the Employment Occupational Standards
Council, EOSC) produced competencies and
standards for the personnel function. This was in
response to research among chief executive officers
and other senior managers (who were not human
resource specialists) who felt that, in general, the
personnel function was not delivering things of
organisational importance.

The National Health Service Training Division
(NHSTD) then used the PSLB standards as the basis
of a survey of over 450 managers and 110 personnel
practitioners in 18 NHS Trusts. As part of this
project, Neil Offley, personnel director of Hinchin-
brooke Health Care NHS Trust, carried out a survey
within his own Trust. He identified a number of key
areas that were important for the future of the Trust,
but in which personnel's current capability was seen
as low. These key areas were:

■ contributing to the overall strategy of the
  organisation
■ developing and maintaining an appropriate
  personnel strategy to support the overall strategy
  of the organisation
■ facilitating external relations
■ developing and maintaining workforce-planning
  to support current and future requirements
■ enhancing individual and group performance
■ developing a reward strategy
■ developing and maintaining employee
  commitment in times of change
■ assessing the needs and opportunities for service
  provision
■ marketing, monitoring and evaluating services.

This was followed by dialogue between line managers
and the personnel department to agree on their

relative roles, ie in light of the survey findings, deciding what the personnel function should be doing and where line managers should be taking responsibility. As a result, a personnel strategy was agreed by the Trust board and a new service agreement was drawn up.

The next stage in the process was to carry out an activity study to find out how personnel staff currently spent their time. (This was done using bar codes for each of the various PSLB areas, scored by use of a light pen.) The 'gap' thus highlighted between current activity and the new service agreement formed the basis for changes within the personnel function, and for a number of retraining initiatives. This study, focusing on establishing effectiveness measures, was carried out with three other NHS Trusts (West Suffolk, Kings Lynn & Wisbech, and Frimley Park), with support from the NHS executive and NHSTD.

Teamworking competencies and skills

Having taken a strategic look at the team – its stages of development and how it is performing when viewed by outsiders such as customers and suppliers – we shall now look at needs within the team.

Teamworking competencies required at each stage

Research and experience has shown that certain skills tend to come into play at each stage of a team's development. Given the overall profile, as described earlier, you can thus get a good idea of some of the team's learning needs. Table 24 shows some of these skills. They are in fact additive – ie you must not, when moving to the next stage, leave behind the skills that have already proved useful, but must contrive to use those *and* add the next set.

Table 24

TEAMWORKING COMPETENCIES AT EACH STAGE OF A TEAM'S DEVELOPMENT

Stages	Teamworking competencies	Levels of performance and need
0: getting ready	Briefing, listening, questioning, allaying fears Obtaining resources Networking Recruiting	
1: getting started	As stage 0, plus: Instructing, making specifications, setting targets, clarifying operational definitions Running meetings, briefings Planning ahead, setting goals Reviewing, evaluating Confronting, challenging, being assertive Supporting, listening, showing empathy Collecting data, gathering detailed information, collecting stories, cases, examples Analysing data, finding essential meaning, interpreting, summarising	I_1: implementing
2: getting going	As stages 0 – 1, plus: Using investigative procedures, causal analysis Team decision-making processes Assertiveness, raising issues, making presentations, presenting cases, supporting, challenging, handling disagreements Reviewing	
3: getting results	As stages 0 – 2, plus: Setting and working to performance targets Running special project meetings eg quality improvement teams Performance improvement methods – collecting data, analysis, flow-charting, fishbone, Pareto, control charts	I_2: improving
4: getting together	As stages 0 – 3, plus: Giving and receiving feedback (positive and negative) Influencing skills Handling diversity Being aware of assumptions Dialoguing	I_3: innovating
5: getting through	As stage 0 – 4, plus: Delegation, mandating procedures for team decision-making Positivity Learning to learn, reviewing, monitoring, evaluating	

X: getting on with others	As other stages, plus: Customer-mapping, role negotiation, bargaining

6: ending	As other stages, plus: Reflecting, reviewing, acknowledging, celebrating Dealing with loss

In the BICC case described in Chapter 1, it was very noticeable how the teams moved through the various stages, with visible changes at each stage. The changes were as follows:

Stage 0: getting ready

▪ Focusing on the business imperative (in this case survival of the plant).
▪ New salary system – single status agreement.
▪ Team leaders appointed.

Stage 1: getting started

▪ Free expression of concerns and fears as well as hopes and expectations about teamworking.
▪ Open discussion and building a picture of what teamworking would be like (no standard blueprint); then an enthusiastic launch.

Stage 2: getting going

▪ Basic procedures established for operational arrangements, eg shift handovers.
▪ Groundrules drawn up for teamworking..
▪ Information supplied to teams on scheduling, targets, etc.
▪ Team left to make own arrangements for machine allocation, etc.
▪ Increased flexibility of working; multiskill training.
▪ Team meetings held on a regular basis; action taken on points raised.

Stage 3: getting results

▪ Priority areas for improvement identified by team members.
▪ Teams trained in improvement tools and techniques.

- Quality improvement projects initiated.
- Outcomes measured, and results recorded and disseminated.

Stage 4: getting together

- Team members assisting one another, standing in, co-operating – without being directed.
- Decisions made more quickly; better decisions made (emphasis on implementation).
- Team leaders and members take up issues directly with senior management.
- Hitherto 'secret' commercial information supplied to teams.
- Teams given responsibility for own budgets.

Stage 5: getting through

- Suggestions for new ways of working, and new rules and moves towards 'self-managed' teamworking structure.
- Teams run their meetings, take action, keep records, and supply information.
- Personal development training established.
- Visits to other organisations.

Stage X: getting on with others

- Intershift and production meetings held; actions followed through.
- Customer-mapping and supplier-mapping lead to improved relationships.

Basic team skills

You may recognise some of the teamworking skills in Table 24, especially those under stage 1 (which are, of course, needed in all the other stages – remember they are

Table 25

BEHAVIOUR ANALYSIS: DEFINITIONS AND EXAMPLES

	Behaviour category	Definition	Examples
R E L A T I O N S H I P S	*Asserting yourself*	A behaviour that puts yourself forward to make a contribution, suggest something, or make a comment. This can be done by: ▪ showing your feelings ▪ supporting ▪ getting noticed ▪ speaking out ▪ shutting others out – interrupting.	'I'm not happy that I haven't said anything yet.' 'Can I say something?' 'What I want to say is...' 'We've heard enough from you. It's my turn now.' 'I feel unhappy about the way we are handling this.'
	Supporting others	A behaviour that supports the contribution and involvement of someone else. This can be done by: ▪ bringing someone else in ▪ supporting what he or she says ▪ agreeing with him or her ▪ building on what he or she has said.	'Could we hear what John has to say?' 'I think that's an excellent suggestion.' 'I agree that's what we should do.' 'That's a good idea; we could do it if we moved the office around.' 'What Gloria says makes me realise that...'
C O N T E N T	*Forming concepts*	A behaviour that pulls together information and ideas already put forward. This can be done by: ▪ analysing data ▪ showing or generating pictures, models, concepts, meaning ▪ generalising ▪ summarising data ▪ testing understanding of concepts.	'This is how I see things fitting together.' 'Item 1 links with item 2.' 'From all that's been said I think there are two main points.' 'The underlying theme here appears to be...'
	Giving and seeking information	A behaviour that takes an ideas and fills out the detail. This can be done by giving or seeking: ▪ facts, clarification ▪ examples, illustrations ▪ explanation of how things work out in practice ▪ detailed stories.	'There are at least five ways of doing that.' 'Chris has done it already by...' 'The stores department did it by cutting out overtime.' 'If we do that, the loss figures will go down.'
P R O C E D U R E S	*Moving on*	A behaviour that moves things on in order to make progress towards objectives. This can be done by: ▪ making proposals and suggestions about procedure ▪ setting out plans ▪ designing a way of working.	'I think we should take a vote.' 'Let's deal with that after item six on the agenda.' 'I suggest we spend 10 minutes on each item.' 'We could look at item two before item one.' 'We should begin with the details before moving on to specifics.'
	Looking back	A behaviour that reviews what has happened – progress and difficulties – and learns from the experience. This can be done by: ▪ summarising decisions ▪ testing understanding of decisions.	'We have dealt with the first half of the agenda.' 'We have agreed to take legal action by the end of May.' 'Can I just check that we all understand the same thing here?'

Table 26

BEHAVIOUR ANALYSIS: CHECK-SHEET

Team activity: Project Meeting   **Date**: 11 March 1996

Behaviour category	John	Jayme	Chris	Harri	Gloria	Roger	Clint	Total	%
RELATIONSHIPS *Asserting yourself* ■ showing your feelings ■ getting noticed ■ speaking out ■ shutting others out – interrupting ■ challenging	2	10	3	2	7	1	1	26	7.93
Supporting others ■ bringing someone else in ■ supporting what he or she says ■ agreeing with him or her ■ building on what he or she has said	0	3			12	0	3	18	5.49
CONTENT *Forming concepts* ■ analysing data ■ showing or generating pictures, models, concepts, meaning ■ generalising ■ summarising data ■ testing understanding of concepts	1	2			1	2	3	9	2.74
Seeking information ■ seeking facts, clarification	12	3	7	6	2	3	1	34	10.36
Giving information ■ giving examples, illustrations ■ explanation of how things work out in practice ■ detailed stories	44	52	20	7	3	7	57	190	57.93
PROCEDURES *Moving on* ■ making proposals and suggestions about procedure ■ setting out plans ■ designing a way of working	1	7	8	2	8	1	3	30	9.15
Looking back ■ summarising decisions ■ testing understanding of decisions	2	5	3	1	6	2	2	21	6.40
Total	62	82	41	18	39	16	70	328	
%	18.90	25.00	12.50	5.49	11.89	4.88	21.34		100.00

additive). They are in fact the same skills that we identified in Chapter 3 – the 'star cluster' of skills involved in ITN (see figure 9, page 58).

Table 25 (on page 166) shows them in expressions more directly associated with team meetings.

We consider the skills outlined in Table 24 to be so basic that we often use them early on in working with teams: they form the basis for a behaviour analysis check-sheet that enables us to analyse meetings. Table 25 defines and gives examples of the relevant behaviour categories. Table 26 (on page 167), meanwhile, shows how you would use these categories in a meeting. You will see that it consists of simply a brief outline of the six main clusters, with columns for each team member. As a trainer or facilitator, your role is to observe the team meeting and place a check-mark in the appropriate place (ie category and person) whenever someone speaks. If a person speaks for more than 10 consecutive seconds, then this counts as separate contribution.

Table 26 includes scores from a particular meeting. You will notice that a lot of contributors were classified as *giving information*. This is often the case. As a team develops through the stages, however, the balance will tend to shift towards behaviours with more emphasis on *procedures* and *relationships*. Again, although *content* will often still dominate, in later stages there will be less *giving information* and more *forming concepts*.

Clearly, some people contributed – or at least spoke – a lot more than others. The nature of contributions from different people varied, too. These observations can all be explored, with subsequent learning for the team as a whole and for individual members. With some practice you should become quite confident in using this tool and in feeding the data back to the group. Our experience is that if there are more than eight team members, you will need another observer to score half the group: eight is enough for one person!

The drawback of the method is that it really allows for verbal interventions only. Gestures and so on tend not to get scored, although you may want to try to include these. You will also have to get used to interpreting tone of voice, emphasis, and the like when deciding which category a particular contribution should go in, because so often 'it's not what you say but the way that you say it' that counts.

This technique is, of course, used in meetings. But do not forget that the behaviours themselves extend beyond meetings into whatever the team members are doing as part of the team. This includes occasions when they are working separately – say in different offices on their aspect of the team's task.

In brief

This chapter has focused on training needs arising from the activities of groups and teams – an increasingly important focus for organisational performance enhancement and individual development. Many teamworking initiatives are being taken by organisations of all kinds. Groups and teams can be seen as a vital link between the individual and the organisation, and initiatives taken at this level can act as a catalyst for the development of both.

We began by using a stage model to highlight training needs that occur at different levels. These training needs will change character as the team (or the teamworking system) matures, and therefore this will require a more developmental or advanced approach, one commensurate with I_1, I_2 and I_3 performance and learning requirements. In order to provide practical tools for readers to work with, the stage model has been translated into a diagnostic exercise.

We then described five further team tools of a strategic nature:

■ U-procedure – a form of team biography process

- SWOT analysis – strengths, weaknesses, opportunities, and threats
- role negotiation – for working on intergroup relationships
- customer- and supplier-mapping – again focusing on the vital area of relationship diagnosis enhancement
- the functional audit – looking at roles and functions of large groups (in this case a whole personnel function).

Specific team training needs can then be identified using a competence-based approach. This makes training needs more specific, precise and 'trainable'. To illustrate how this approach works out in practice we can return to the BICC case example in Chapter 1.

A further important area of team-training needs is revealed when we use a behavioural approach. The star cluster of skills and behaviours provides us with an important diagnostic tool, as well as a way of thinking about specific team actions and behaviours.

Reference

HARRISON R 'Role Negotiation', in R Harrison (ed.), *The Collected Papers of Roger Harrison*. Maidenhead; McGraw-Hill, 1995, pp42–54.

9

Focusing on
Individual Needs

In this chapter we shall focus on the shaded area in Table 27. In fact, as we shall see, much of what we have described about teams in earlier chapters can be modified for use with individuals.

Table 27

FOCUS OF CHAPTER 9

Area of need / Level of business benefit	Organisational	Group	Individual
I_1: Implementing – doing things well	Meeting current organisational objectives	Working together to meet existing targets and standards	Being competent at the level of existing requirements
I_2: Improving – doing things better	Setting higher objectives and reaching them	Continuous improvement teams	Having and using systematic, continuous improvement skills and processes
I_3: Innovating – doing new and better things	Changing objectives and strategies	Working across boundaries to create new relationships and new products and services	Being able to work differently and more creatively with a shared sense of purpose

'TWI training plan' approach

'Training Within Industry' (TWI) was a programme introduced into the UK in the 1950s. Sponsored by the then Ministry of Labour (don't these terms have an old-fashioned ring about them!), it consisted of a number of courses for supervisors, one of which – job instruction – included the training plan, a simple yet effective way of linking individual and departmental training needs.

The essence of the plan is as follows. A chart is drawn up (Table 28) listing the departmental tasks, skills, or processes down one side, and the names of the individuals across the top. Provision is also made for indicating the departmental requirement – in this case, for the number of people needed to be of a high standard at each task.

The method is quite simple. An estimate of each person's proficiency in each task is entered in the corresponding cell. In this case we are using a simple three-part 'scale':

blank	not at all proficient
●	fairly proficient
●●	highly proficient

Of course, these categories may need further elaboration or definition, but in many cases, simple and relatively crude though it may be, this approach can work surprisingly well.

Once the proficiencies have been estimated they can be compared with the departmental requirements. From this, specific training plans can be drawn up, to meet departmental needs, ensure that we are not dangerously or unfairly dependent on a particular individual to carry out much of the more skilled work, and provide each person with the opportunity to acquire an extensive range of competencies.

This basic approach can be used in other settings. For example, the training and quality unit of a major blue-

Table 28

'TRAINING PLAN'

Tasks/skills/processes	Individuals					Departmental requirement [••] (no. of people required at this standard)	Requirement satisfied?
	Pat	Hilary	Yasmin	Donna	David		
Using electric typewriter	••	••	•		•	2	Yes
Using basic word-processor	••	••	•		•	5	No
Using desk-top publisher	•	••	•			4	No
Using graphics package					••	2	No
Typing from dictaphone	•		•			2	No
Taking shorthand			••	•		3	No

chip organisation has this four-point categorisation:

Level 1:
understand –   able to describe to a third party 'what it is; what the policy or strategy is; where it fits in with other training and quality products and services; who is responsible'.

Level 2: active
support   –   contributes to the design or development of a training or quality product or service by supplying information, time, or other resource; can deliver training; attends regular briefings; can communicate and sell the product or service to a third party.

Level 3: able to
stand in   –   can cover for the 'responsible' person (see below) in his or her absence; for example, can deliver training or workshops; set up new courses; run the operation.

Level 4:
responsible – the process owner for the design and delivery of a product or service; runs the operation; plans and controls the budget and staffing resources; produces effectiveness measures; is part of a project team on new policies and product specifications.

Interestingly enough, there is a fairly close match with the modes framework here:

Level 1: understand   Modes 1 to 3

Level 2: active support   Modes 1 to 4

Level 3: able to stand in   Modes 1 to 5, some 6

Level 4: responsible   Modes 1 to 7

The organisation uses this categorisation in a way very similar to the 'training plan'. Thus, departmental needs are compared with the proficiency level of each member, and development plans made to ensure departmental needs are met and that individuals are given the chance to acquire new skills and learn new sets of tasks.

Using Objective Data

To complete the training plan – either literally or metaphorically – we sometimes need objective data to help determine current proficiency levels. We have already discovered how to do this (see Chapters 4 and 5). For convenience, this information is summarised here, a full explanation being given in those chapters:

1   Define the part of the organisation you are working in. If necessary, chart it so as to get an overall picture of what is involved.

2   If necessary, collect more data.

3   Analyse the data, possibly using control charts, to identify areas of poor performance.

4   Find out the causes of the poor performance, which may include needs for training.

5   Prioritise the causes.

6   Propose and prioritise possible solutions, which may include individual training.

Competency frameworks and job analysis

The training plan approach used a set of tasks, abilities, or skills against which individual proficiency was measured, A generic term for these tasks and so on is *competencies*.

Where does the appropriate competency framework came from? In many cases it will be through a form of job analysis, where the job or role under consideration is broken down into a number of tasks and procedures. The skills, knowledge, and perhaps attitudes and values required to carry out the tasks are then identified.

In broad terms job analysis may involve a combination of observation; interviews with jobholders, bosses, subordinates, customers, peers, and trainers, either individually or in groups; questionnaires; reference to documents, manuals, and procedures; and perhaps trying to do the job yourself. There are a number of methods of collating, analysing, and presenting data thus obtained. In their useful book, Pearn and Kandola (1993) describe 18 such methods.

Job analysis may be used in conjunction with published 'standards'. These are, in effect, frameworks of competencies that have been developed and published for specific jobs. The UK government has stated that in principle there will be such standards for every job or occupation in the country. For example, the Institute of Personnel and Development distributes what are referred to as *Personnel Standards*. These consist of a map of five main personnel functions – used, incidentally, in the functional audit described in Chapter 8 – each of which is then further subdivided. A brief extract illustrates the principle:

A. Five main functions:

    1 strategy and organisation

    2 resourcing

    3 development

    4 reward management

    5 employee relations.

B. Take as an example Function 3 (development). This is now divided into:

    1 performance development strategy

    2 performance planning and review

    3 promotion of training

    4 long-term individual development

    5 team development

    6 equality of opportunity

    7 support for development.

C. Each of these is further divided; we shall take as an example item 6 – equality of opportunity. This requires people to:

    1 design and select processes for monitoring and facilitating equal opportunities

    2 communicate and gain support for monitoring and facilitating equal opportunities across a significant part of the organisation

    3 implement processes for the promotion of equal opportunities across a significant part of the organisation

    4 Monitor and evaluate equal opportunities across a significant part of the organisation.

D. The standards then go into further detail about the knowledge, understanding and skills required to carry out the above.

These standards are, of course, generic. Many organisations

like to modify or customise them for their own use. Not only does this ensure a high degree of relevance, but usually people are more likely to be committed to an in-house version.

The modes of learning from Chapter 1 can also be used for indicating standards because there are some generic 'modal' competencies associated with each mode that are often not included in standard competency manuals. This is particularly true for working in modes 4 to 7 (see Table 29).

Table 29

GENERIC LEARNING NEEDS FOR MODES 4 TO 7

Mode	Learning need	Training in these techniques can help meet need
4 Experiencing	Learning to make one's own meaning from experiences; creating or discovering one's own understanding	Having experiences, reflecting, forming new ideas, trying out
5 Experimenting	Learning to find out, in a systematic way, more about something by hypothesising, carrying out carefully planned experiments or pilot projects, and analysing and reviewing the results of these	Systematically structuring experiences – improvement tools such as surveys, flow charts, brainstorming, fishbone, Pareto, nominal group technique, correlation analysis, control charts
6 Connecting	Learning to see systemically – wholes, connections, patterns, interdependencies; hence to empathise, identify with others, acknowledge and value diversity	Reflecting, seeking patterns, themes, and assumptions; dialogue; relationship-mapping; role negotiation; continuous improvement tools
7 Dedicating	Learning to recognise and commit oneself to one's purpose in life, in the sense of joining with others to do something in and for the external world.	U-procedure, whole-system interventions

Using feedback from others

Much identification of individual needs is through feedback from others. Appraisal is probably the most widespread approach to this.

The appraisal process

The appraisal process is usually related either to a competency framework, like that just described, or to a set of tasks and goals that were agreed between the appraiser and appraisee. (What an ugly word! From now on we will use 'learner'.) Usually some form of rating scale is then used. Typically this may consist of a number of points on a scale, such as:

Competence   Teamwork
cluster:

Behaviour: Open-minded – encourages people to
               state their opinions even when these
               differ from appraiser's own

Scale:

1 2 3 4 5 6 7

Almost   Almost
always   never

An alternative, which requires more careful construction, gives quite detailed descriptions for the scale points. Greatrex and Phillips (1989) give an example from BP concerning four main competence clusters:

- *Achievement orientation*: personal drive, organisational drive, impact, communication
- *People-orientation*: awareness of others, team management, persuasiveness
- *Judgement*: analytical power, strategic thinking, commercial judgment
- *Situational flexibility*: adaptive orientation.

Going into a little more detail, one of the above competencies may be described thus:

Personal drive Self-confident and assertive drive to win, with decisiveness and resilience.

❶	❷	❸	❹	❺
Decisive even under pressure; assertive and tough-minded in arguing his or her case; very self-confident; shrugs off setbacks	Will commit him- or herself to definite opinions; determined to be heard; can come back strongly if attached	May reserve judgement where uncertain, but stands firm on important points; aims for compromise; fairly resilient	Avoids taking rapid decisions; takes an impartial co-ordinator role rather than push own ideas	Does not pursue his or her points; goes along with the group; allows criticism or setbacks to deter him or her

+ Indicators:

■ tough-minded driving style; pushes to get own way
■ persistent in arguing points
■ concerned to get solution he or she owns
■ can confront others when important
■ makes clear decisions when required
■ commits self to definite opinions
■ resilient to setbacks
■ enjoys challenge; can accept mistakes
■ maintains confidence

– Indicators:

■ rather soft or 'nice'
■ does not pursue his or her points
■ does not like confronting others
■ inclined to give way if attacked
■ lets others make the decisions
■ backs off from giving definite view
■ reacts emotionally to setbacks
■ worried about mistakes
■ lacks confidence; appears uncertain

The appraiser is usually the learner's immediate line manager, although sometimes it is someone at the next higher level. Although in theory it is a strictly logical, rational process, it is very easy for bias to set in. Terry Gillen's valuable book (1995) suggests four main types of such bias, along with suggested preventive action. These are reproduced here in abridged form as Table 30 (on page 180).

Another valuable book that addresses the strengths and weaknesses of appraisal is that by Clive Fletcher (1993). One particular area of controversy is that of linking appraisal to reward through performance-related pay

Table 30

MAIN TYPES OF BIAS IN APPRAISAL
(from Gillen 1995)

Main types of bias	Preventive action
Horns and halo Someone does something particularly bad or particularly good and we allow the impression we gained at the time to colour our judgement of them thereafter.	Base appraisal on actual performance against predefined criteria.
'Recency' Allowing recent events to outweigh less recent events. It is hardly any wonder that recent events carry more weight in our minds than older ones. Yet something that happened 11 months ago should carry the same weight in our assessment as something that happened last week.	Use records of regular informal appraisals rather than rely on memory.
Sexual and racial discrimination A report published by the Institute of Manpower Studies and the Equal Opportunities Commission in 1992 pointed to the potential for appraisers to allow gender stereotyping to influence their assessment of performance. Other sources have pointed towards similar concerns over racial stereotyping, and even a tendency to mark physically attractive people (of either sex) more generously than their less attractive colleagues!	Base appraisal on actual performance against predefined criteria. Question your own values.
Organisation culture bias In some organisations technical excellence is prized; in others, it is commitment measured by long hours. Some managers prize initiative others obedience, and some would prefer that every new recruit was a clone of themselves. It is worth considering your own organisation and personal likes and dislikes.	Base appraisal on actual performance against predefined criteria. Question your own values.

(PRP). The current state of play here seems that, increasingly, PRP is being seen as a hindrance to learning, development, and long-term performance, although it is still used by a large number of organisations.

360° feedback

Traditional appraisal fits very well with the rational and bureaucratic phases of an organisation, as described in Chapter 7. Increasingly, however, as organisations enter the shake-up or even the integrated phases, flatter structures, self-management and empowerment, and an emphasis on customers rather than on bosses begin to give rise to the need for something more flexible and holistic. This is where 360° feedback comes in.

First of all, what is it? Basically, the 360° aspect refers to the fact that learners get feedback, usually on some form of rating scale, from a *range* of sources, which may include their line manager, peers, subordinates, and customers. They usually rate themselves as well, and much of the value of the feedback often lies in comparing the data from these different sources. Another key feature of the approach used by pioneers in this field, Pilat UK, is that it involves measures of *importance* as well as *performance* for each identified competence of behaviour. (Figure 39 on page 182 shows a sample of this; the numbers there refer to the various competencies being assessed.) The principle has been illustrated several times already in this book, for it allows prioritising perceived weaknesses (top left-hand quadrant) as well as identifying useful strengths to build on (top right-hand quadrant). Obviously such data can be presented according to the specific source (peer, subordinate, customer) or on an aggregated basis.

Pilat UK see four main reasons for the increasing use of this approach to feedback (Pilat UK 1995):

1 Self-managed learning

Many organisations now acknowledge that the most effective training and development are those managed by the individual. This can produce more accurate diagnosis of needs, faster response, clearer focus to the activity, increased commitment, and more cost-effective solutions. However, the quality of the solution will always depend

Figure 39

PRINT-OUT FROM 360° FEEDBACK

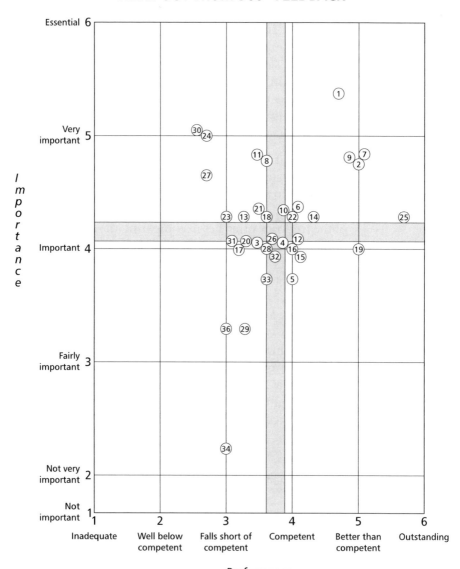

on the quality of the diagnosis of need. Feedback from others on specific aspects of performance has been found to be extremely useful in this respect.

2 Need for support for quality management

Many organisations have implemented total quality management (TQM) only to find that the momentum deteriorates as individuals find it increasingly difficult to identify issues. Continuous improvement requires continuous measurement of the gap between actual performance and customer requirements. Feedback processes, especially from internal and external clients, offer individuals the opportunity to receive feedback on the 'soft issues' that are key to successful TQM initiatives.

3 Flatter structures/empowerment

The move to flatter structures demands that individuals are empowered to act. Consequently, individuals need higher-level skills and processes in order to adapt to this devolved decision-making. Feedback processes have to reflect these changes. First, new sources of feedback have to be considered, because the line manager is now not always best placed to observe behaviour. Secondly, the feedback processes also have to respond to the change by providing individuals with the opportunity to obtain feedback directly and to take responsibility for decisions based on it.

4 Teamworking, cross-functional working and matrix structures

The need for flexibility and responsiveness to the market-place, in addition to the need to reduce labour costs, has also encouraged many organisations to implement teamworking; to increase the use of cross-functional working; and to implement matrix (multiboss) structures. If genuine teamworking is implemented, there is only one source of information on how each team member is performing: other team members. In the case of cross-functional working, the source of information is the individuals with whom the person operates – the peers, colleagues and clients – who know best *how* he or she operates. In the case of matrix structures, each boss is likely to observe different aspects of an individual's performance or behaviour. Hence multisource assessment or feedback becomes very valuable.

Customer-mapping and role negotiation

In Chapter 8 we saw how these techniques can be used for feedback to a team. They can also be used by individuals talking with their own customers and suppliers (who may be other team members, or from outside the team) and doing role negotiation with them.

Linda Honold, a consultant to one of America's most successful quality and learning organisations, Johnsonville Foods, describes one way in which this process works well (Honold 1994).

> In the office there are six individuals who do word processing for a variety of people throughout the company. It is a team approach, so no one of them works for any individual; rather, work comes to the team and they divide it up depending on each person's workload at the time.

> A contract is developed whereby the team agrees that they will achieve an average turnover time of 24 hours, and that this will be a six-month goal. Each person develops a personal contract to feed into the team contract. One member decides that if she knew the ins and outs of the word processing program better, she could reduce her turn-around time. Another determines that external distractions are what keep him from providing the best performance. The key is that each individual has a role to play in helping the team achieve its goal.

> At the end of each month, the team resubmits the contract to their customers with the question, 'Are

we making progress towards our ultimate goal?' The feedback is then brought into a team meeting in which each person relates how he or she is doing in their personal part of the contract. Because they are reporting back to their peers on a monthly basis, performance becomes completely visible. If one person is not following through on the contract, he or she has no choice but to admit it to the rest of the group. If one person is doing an exemplary job of meeting his or her part of the contract, positive feedback is given by his or her peers. The peers provide reinforcement.

Results of performance contracting are that internal customers are better serviced and that peers talk to one another about performance. In addition, 'politicking' is reduced because of the openness of communication, and individuals throughout the organisation learn. The end-user, the customer, ultimately is being served better.

Feedback from oneself

We have seen that 360° feedback usually includes some self-assessment. It is possible of course to do the latter on its own, without data from others. This takes us into the area of self-development, (see *Cultivating Self-Development*, by D Megginson and V Whitaker to be published by the IPD in 1996). Here we shall note just two approaches to self-assessment:

- using an open-ended method
- using a framework of competencies.

Open-ended self-assessment: incident analysis

This method was developed by Boydell and Leary (1993). The process is as follows:

1   Think of two occasions when, in your opinion, you did something really well. (You may find it most useful

if you confine yourself to achievements at work –
although this is not essential.) What happened?

2 Who was involved?

3 What were you thinking at the time? How did you
   feel?

4 What did you want to do, and what not to do?

5 What did you do?

6 Now do the same for two occasions when things went
   wrong – when you felt you did not do yourself justice.
   What happened?

7 Who was involved?

8 What were you thinking at the time? How did you
   feel?

9 What did you want to do, and what not to do?

10 What did you do?

11 Now, looking back over these incidents, what do they
    tell you about your development needs?

Using a framework of competencies for self-assessment

Clearly, what you need here is a particular set of
competencies. You can then assess yourself against them
in a variety of ways, including:

■ rating your current performance

■ rating the importance of each competency in your
   current job

■ rating the importance of each competency for a job to
   which you aspire

■ comparing your performance ratings with one or both
   of those for importance either by simple subtraction
   or, as we showed for the modes in Chapter 8, by taking
   the ratio of performance to importance (that is,
   dividing the performance score by the importance
   score).

Once you have carried out this assessment you can then
decide what it tells you about your development needs.

Of course, 360° feedback usually includes self-assessment, as well as data from others. Indeed, one of its main features is the ability to compare your self-rating with those from other sources, and then to explore what any differences may mean.

In brief

This chapter has focused on identifying individual needs. In addition to techniques such as 'the training plan' much of what has been described earlier in this book may be used. For example, the process of analysing needs, described in detail in Chapter 5, very often highlights areas of individual need.

Many approaches to identifying individual needs start from a basis of a competency framework, which may be organisation-specific or based on an occupational standard. In addition, certain generic needs are associated with specific modes, especially modes 4 to 7.

We looked at feedback from others, particularly appraisal and its evolved form, 360° feedback. We also stressed the importance of separating feedback for learning and development from decisions about rewards.

We then showed how customer-mapping and role negotiation can also be used at the individual level, and finally we described briefly two methods of self-diagnosis.

References

BOYDELL TH AND LEARY M *Personal Effectiveness.* Henley-on-Thames; Henley Distance Learning (HDL Training and Development), 1993.

FLETCHER C *Appraisal.* London; Institute of Personnel Management, 1993.

GILLEN T *The Appraisal Discussion.* London; Institute of Personnel and Development, 1995.

GREATREX J AND PHILLIPS P 'Oiling the Wheels of Competence', *Personnel Management,* August 1989, pp36–9.

PEARN M AND KANDOLA R *Job Analysis*. London; 2nd edition, Institute of Personnel Management, 1993.

PILAT UK. *360° Feedback™: The key principles.* London; Pilat UK, 1995.

Appendix: Identifying Training Needs and Investors In People

Many trainers may well find themselves involved in Investors In People (IIP), a government-led initiative to improve the quality of training and human resources management by linking them firmly with business performance and strategy. Organisations that meet certain specified standards gain the IIP award.

In this Appendix we include a summary of the IIP scheme, set out in a way that, we hope, provides guidelines for IIP-related identification of training needs (ITN).

The processes in an IIP scheme overlap substantially with those with which we have been concerned under the heading of ITN. This chapter will show how the various techniques and processes of ITN can be used not only for the benefit of the organisation but also for achieving an IIP award.

If we begin by examining the antecedents of and philosophy behind IIP we can immediately see why the scheme has so much potential, for it is based on many of the training and learning ideas that we have used as the foundations for this book.

Some of the thinking behind IIP and its link with ITN

The Government White Paper *Employment in the 1990s* expressed concerns over the low level of investment in training in the UK and the difficulties involved in proving the link between training and organisational success –

issues of central concern in this book. The National Training Task Force was subsequently set up to consult with the business community and to examine current best practices (an example of benchmarking). IIP is a national scheme established to respond to the challenge of insufficient training investment in the following ways:

■ *by establishing the concept of people as an investment as the centrepiece of IIP*. It is often said by organisations that 'people are our most valuable asset', but all too often only lipservice is paid to this concept. IIP emphasises that people are, in fact, the one truly sustainable source of competitive advantage.

■ *by focusing schemes on performance enhancement*. As we have seen, this will be at three possible levels I_1 – implementing; I_2 – improving; I_3 – innovating. Organisations striving for extra competitiveness and world-class status will need to consider setting up more sophisticated training systems. The standards required by IIP take this into consideration and are therefore set at a high level.

Further details on IIP standards can be obtained from local Training and Enterprise Councils, which are responsible for running IIP Schemes. Advisers are appointed to help organisations work towards IIP standards, while assessors check whether the requirements have been met.

Guidance for IIP

In order to see clearly what IIP is about we shall assume that your organisation has committed itself to working towards achieving the award. What will advisers and assessors be looking for?

One of the first principles of IIP is that all evidence presented should allow for consistent and systematic review. This means that the whole training process (including, of course, ITN) should be visible, clearly understood by all those involved, and open to assessment, review, and evaluation. The IIP format therefore provides us with two important sources of guidance and experience in terms of ITN: national standards and an assessment or ITN process.

National standards

National standards for the setting up of a training system in an organisation are based on the following principles and values:

▮ People are the key to higher productivity, better quality, customer responsiveness, and flexibility or speed of response.

▮ The successful organisations of the 1990s will be those that release the full potential of their people.

▮ Training should be seen as an investment, not just a cost.

From the above a number of key features of a successful IIP training system emerge. These are:

▮ making a commitment to investing in people

▮ using a planned approach to all aspects of training, beginning with ITN

▮ starting with business objectives, using the training and development of people to deliver measurable benefits to the organisation.

So, an Investor in People:

1   makes a public commitment from the top to develop all employees to achieve the business objectives

2   regularly reviews the training and development needs of all its employees

3   takes action to train and develop individuals on recruitment and throughout their employment

4   evaluates the investment in training and development to assess achievement and improve future performance.

These last four statements are known as *the IIP standards* or *principles*.

An assessment or ITN process

Although designed to be used by trained and experienced IIP assessors, and assessment or ITN process can also be followed as a guideline by anyone undertaking an ITN exercise. The IIP process involves:

Commitment	– public, open, and in writing
Self-assessment	– against the standards by the organisation (with help from outside advisors)
Action plan	– to bridge gaps, collect evidence, and decide who will do what, where, and when

Implementation of action plan:

application for assessment	– when the action plan has been implemented and standards reached assessment by a qualified external assessor
recognition	– as an IIP

then

Continuous improvement

Reassessment	– every three years

In order to make the above ITN/IIP cycle happen in a way that involves and engages everyone in the proceedings, a number of further criteria have to be met. These are the need to:

▮ get and keep everyone on board

▮ go at your own pace – but keep up the momentum

- involve everyone as actively as possible
- never lose sight of the potential benefits
- evaluate, monitor, and collect evidence as you go along and at every opportunity
- keep the paperwork and bureaucracy to a minimum
- use whatever support services are around.

IIP assessment procedure

Each of the four IIP standards or principles already described is broken down into a number of assessment indicators – things that the assessor looks for to check that the principles have been translated into practical action, supported by typical evidence. These are shown in Table 31 (on pages 195–7).

The White House case: ITN as a development process

To illustrate how an IIP-based ITN process works, we have taken the example of a small organisation recently assessed against the IIP standards. We shall concentrate on how the staff and management experienced the initial diagnostic assessment stages.

> The White House is a care home for the elderly on the outskirts of Sheffield with 15 residents and 20 staff. As part of her development, one of the two assistant managers has taken on special responsibilities for introducing IIP to the organisation, working closely with management and staff colleagues.
>
> A great deal of work had been carried out in improving systems and generally focusing on training needs before it was decided to commit the organisation to IIP.
> The management and staff welcomed the opportunity for receiving the outside opinion and view that

would be provided by an experienced and qualified IIP adviser appointed by the local Training and Enterprise Council (TEC). After spending a few days at the White House, carrying out a thorough investigation and discussion with all management, staff, and residents the adviser produced a report (summarised in Table 32, pages 198–9). As can be seen, this included what had been done already, any suggested further action required to bridge the gap between current performance and IIP standards, and a few examples of the kind of evidence that would illustrate the standards had been met.

The way in which the staff then proceeded towards gaining the IIP award is beyond the scope of this book. We hope, however, that this short illustration may help some of the many trainers and, indeed, line managers who are themselves working towards the award.

Table 31

IIP STANDARDS, ASSESSMENT INDICATORS AND TYPICAL SUPPORTING EVIDENCE

Standard	Assessment indicators	Typical evidence
1 An *Investor In People* makes a public commitment from the top to develop all employees to achieve its business objectives.	1.1 There is a public commitment from the most senior level within the organisation to develop people.	Mission or vision statement; written plan; letter of commitment; active involvement by the organisation in relevant activities (ITOs, MCI, Business/Education partnerships); National Training Award.
■ Every employer should have a written flexible plan which sets out business goals and targets, considers how employees will contribute to achieving the plan and specifies how development needs in particular will be assessed and met.	1.2 Employees at all levels are aware of the broad aims or vision of the organisation.	Mission or vision statement, expressed in a way that everyone can understand; employee survey; employee representatives' statements; employee-briefing arrangements.
	1.3 There is a written but flexible plan which sets out business goals and targets.	Relevant extracts from plan; evidence that the plan has been reviewed where necessary.
	1.4 The plan identifies broad development needs and specifies how they will be assessed and met.	Relevant extracts from plan; top-level review.
■ Management should develop and communicate to all employees a vision of where the organisation is going and the contribution employees will make to its success, involving employee representatives as appropriate.	1.5 The employer has considered what employees at all levels will contribute to the success of the organisation and has communicated this effectively to them.	Mission or vision statement and what it says about people; employee survey; personal plans.
	1.6 Where representative structures exist, management communicates with employee representatives a vision of where the organisation is going and the contribution employees (and their representatives) will make to its success.	Statement from employee representatives; minutes of joint meetings; material produced locally by employee representatives.
2 An *Investor In People* regularly reviews the training and development needs of all employees.	2.1 The written plan identifies the resources that will be used to meet training and development needs.	Written plan; top-level review.
■ The resources for training and developing employees should be clearly identified in the business plan.	2.2 Training and development needs are regularly reviewed against business objectives.	Written plan; top-level review; training or skills audits with a clear business focus; quality manual for ISO 9000; Total Quality Strategy document.
	2.3 A process exists for regularly reviewing the training and development needs of all employees.	Individual plans; performance appraisal system; top-level review.

(continued on page 196)

Table 31 (continued)

IIP STANDARDS, ASSESSMENT INDICATORS AND TYPICAL SUPPORTING EVIDENCE

Standard	Assessment indicators	Typical evidence
Managers should be responsible for regularly agreeing training and development needs with each employee in the context of business objectives, setting targets and standards linked, where appropriate, to the achievement of National Vocational Qualifications (NVQs) (or relevant units) and in Scotland, Scottish Vocational Qualifications (SVQs).	2.4 Responsibility for developing people is clearly identified throughout the organisation, starting at the top.	Mission or vision statement; job descriptions, plan; top-level review; actions by managers which reflect their responsibilities; quality manual; Total Quality Strategy document.
	2.5 Managers are competent to carry out their responsibilities for developing people.	Job plans; performance appraisal system; training and development actions; use of management development standards; ISO 9000 accreditation.
	2.6 Targets and standards are set for development actions.	Written plan; top-level review; evaluation results; personal plans; quality manual; Company Safety policy.
	2.7 Where appropriate, training targets are linked to achieving external standards, and particularly to NVQ (or SVQ in Scotland).	Training plans; performance appraisals; use of NVQs/ units; ISO 9000 accreditation.
3 An Investor In People takes action to train and develop individuals on recruitment and throughout their employment.	3.1 All new employees are introduced effectively to the organisation and are given the training and development they need to do their jobs.	Appointment process; documented induction programmes; information pack for new joiners; employee survey.
Action should focus on the training needs of all new recruits and on continually developing and improving the skills of existing employees.	3.2 The skills of existing employees are developed in line with business objectives.	Training plans; top-level review; training and development actions; achievement of NVQs.
	3.3 All employees are made aware of the development opportunities open to them.	Employee survey; arrangements for communication with employees; actual communications.
All employees should be encouraged to contribute to identifying and meeting their own job-related development needs.	3.4 All employees are encouraged to help identify and meet their job-related development needs.	Job plans; training and development actions; employee survey; performance appraisal system; existence of learning resource centres; use of open and flexible learning materials.
	3.5 Effective action takes place to achieve the training and development objectives of individuals and the organisation.	Training and development actions; performance appraisals; training records; ISO 9000 accreditation; use of open and flexible learning materials; achievement of NVQs.
	3.6 Managers are actively involved in supporting employees to meet their training and development needs.	Job descriptions or plans; employee survey; performance appraisal system; achievement of management standards.

(continued on page 197)

Table 31 (continued)

IIP STANDARDS, ASSESSMENT INDICATORS AND TYPICAL SUPPORTING EVIDENCE

Standard	Assessment indicators	Typical evidence
4 An **Investor In People** evaluates the investment in training and development to assess achievement and improve future effectiveness.	4.1 The organisation evaluates how its development of people is contributing to business goals and targets.	Top-level review; evaluation studies; consultants' reports; National Training Award applications.
■ The investment, the competence and commitment of employees, and the use made of skills learned should be reviewed at all levels against business goals and targets.	4.2 The organisation evaluates whether its development actions have achieved their objectives.	Evaluation results; performance appraisals; accreditation of NVQs.
	4.3 The outcomes of training and development are evaluated at individual, team and organisational levels.	Employee surveys; skills audits; evaluation results; performance appraisal system.
■ The effectiveness of training and development should be reviewed at the top level and lead to renewed commitment and target-setting.	4.4 Top management understand the broad costs and benefits of developing people.	Written plan; top-level review; evidence of business benefits.
	4.5 The continuing commitment of top management to developing people is communicated to all employees.	Employee communications; employee survey.

Table 32

AN INITIAL DIAGNOSTIC ASSESSMENT AGAINS IIP STANDARDS FOR THE WHITE HOUSE CARE HOME

IIP indi-cators	Where are we now?	Action required	Evidence	Dates
1.1	Commitment shown in practice. No training policy or mission statement to state commitment explicitly.	Make formal IIP commitment to TEC. Draw up training policy.	Letter of commitment. Certificate. Training policy.	
1.2	Staff meetings used to explain business plan. Newsletter published. All staff aware that caring for residents is most important.	Agree mission statement and discuss with all staff. Continue to keep staff informed about the business.	Newsletter. Business plan. Mission statement.	
1.3	There is a 1995–96 business plan setting out clear targets. A summary is included in the newsletter.	Draw up a longer-term strategic plan, covering say the next three to five years.	Strategic plan. Business plan. Summary in newsletter.	
1.4	Already included in the 1995–96 business plan.	Continue to include training and development requirements in future business plans.	1995–96 business plan.	
1.5	All staff have job descriptions. There are regular staff meetings, a newsletter, and employee handbook. All staff know where the business is going and how they fit in.	Continue with existing communication channels and ensure that the newsletter continues to be published regularly.	Job descriptions. Staff meeting minutes. Newsletter. Other communication systems – diary and communications book.	
1.6	There are no representative structures.			
2.1	The budget for training and development is included in the overall financial plan.	Consider calculating staff time for training and development to show the true cost to the home.	Extract from financial plan. Calculation of staff time.	
2.2	Business plan identifies needs and there is training associated with personnel systems. Reviews take place at staff–management (SMT) meetings.	Ensure minuting of SMT meetings where training and development needs are reviewed against business needs.	Personnel training plan. Business plan. SMT meeting minutes. Local authority reports.	
2.3	All staff have had one formal appraisal with the manager. Revised documentation is now ready for the second round of appraisals.	Ensure that the pattern of appraisals is established and complete the second round of appraisals, which will result in personal development plans for staff.	Two sets of appraisal documentation.	
2.4	Managers' job descriptions show responsibilities which were confirmed by staff interviews.	No action required.	Managers' job descriptions.	

(continued opposite)

Table 32 (continued)

AN INITIAL DIAGNOSTIC ASSESSMENT AGAINS IIP STANDARDS FOR THE WHITE HOUSE CARE HOME

IIP indicators	Where are we now?	Action required	Evidence	Dates
2.5	Manager has Certificate in Competence in Residential Care Management and the assistant managers are working towards this. Manager will be an NVQ assessor.	No action required.	Certificates for NVQ assessor and Competence in Residential Care Management.	
2.6	Training is focused and targets often self-evident. Establishing expected outcomes is informal at the moment.	Establish core-training briefing system with appropriate documentation. Ensure intended outcomes of training are clear.	Staff meeting minutes. Pre-training briefing documentation.	
2.7	Two staff studying NVQ Level 2 and two NVQ Level 3. Cook has Food Hygiene Certificate. Manager studying to be an NVQ Assessor.	Continue NVQ programme.	NVQ documentation and certificates. Food Hygiene Certificate.	
3.1	Induction programme and check-list established. Training programme for all staff within first three months. An employee handbook and interviews confirm welcome and support.	No action required.	Employee handbook. Completed induction sheets and check-lists. Training packs and programmes.	
3.2	There are individual training records signed by staff giving details of training, and a lot of evidence of relevant training – first aid, fire, health and safety, lifting and handling.			

I
Index